WANG RENMEI

WANG RENMEI
The Wildcat of Shanghai

Richard J. Meyer

香港大學出版社
HONG KONG UNIVERSITY PRESS

Hong Kong University Press
The University of Hong Kong
Pokfulam Road
Hong Kong
www.hkupress.org

ISBN 978-988-8139-96-5 (*Paperback*)

British Library Cataloguing-in-Publication Data
A catalogue record for this book is available from the British Library.

10 9 8 7 6 5 4 3 2 1

Printed and bound by ColorPrint Production Ltd., Hong Kong, China

Contents

Illustrations

The title song, written by Nie Er, increased Wang's popularity with her recording of the lyrics.

Photo 1.18   Wang Renmei sings "Song of the Fishermen" while her brother helps with the net. He dies at the end of the film and asks his sister to sing it one more time.

Photo 1.19   Wang Renmei with the cast on location in the tiny village of Shipu where they filmed *Song of the Fishermen*. The director could only find a small fishing boat for the shoot which caused many actors to become seasick.

Photo 1.20   Nie Er, famous Chinese composer who wrote the music for *Song of the Fishermen* and other films; his song "March of the Volunteers" became China's national anthem.

Photo 1.21   *Song of the Fishermen* with Wang Renmei as Little Cat, Han Langen as Little Monkey, and Pei Yiwei as the uncle.

Photo 1.22   Wang Renmei as Yan Yuying in the play, *The Song for Returning Spring*. Music was written by Nie Er, with script by Tian Han.

Photo 1.23   Wang Renmei as Ma Nina and Mei Xi as Zhu Dongxin in *The Song of Perpetual Regret*. This was her first film for the newly created Xinhua Enterprises, established by Zhang Shankun.

Photo 1.24   Wu Yonggang became famous when his first film *The Goddess* was considered a masterpiece. He directed Wang Renmei in three films for Xinhua Enterprises, including *Soaring Aspirations, Pirates of the Yellow Sea,* and *Parting from Heaven with Sorrow.*

(All photographs courtesy of the China Film Archive and Qin Yi.)

Foreword

T here are two positions one can adopt when introducing a speaker or an author's work: one can speak or write from a position of authority and expertise, full of knowledge and nuance about the topic, or as a generalist, eager to learn about an area in which he or she has no special knowledge. I have had the pleasure and the honor of introducing Dr. Richard J. Meyer, an accomplished film historian, on numerous occasions, but I have never had a choice about how to do it: I am always in the enviable position of wanting to learn about an area outside my specializations, and I have never been disappointed in how much I have learned or in the delightful manner in which that learning takes place. I am, however, something of a specialist in recognizing well-written, important film scholarship from the perspective of an editor, having spent years editing the film journal *Wide Angle* and then editing several film book anthologies. From that perspective, it is with expertise that I introduce this book.

I met Richie at the justly celebrated Pordenone Silent Film Festival what seems a long time ago, which is only appropriate considering that gathering is devoted to early cinema. He had already distinguished himself in that field by, among other things, having helped to develop the San Francisco Silent Film Festival. Exposure to retrospectives of Keaton, Chaplin, and Griffith during a brief time that I lived in New York became an important factor in my later switching majors in graduate school from English to film, where I had the further privilege of taking a seminar on Griffith from Russell Merritt. I never again, however, lived in places where I had good access and opportunity to pursue that interest. To say I was playing catch-up with Richie in Pordenone would be an understatement.

The same is true with Chinese cinema. Like most film scholars, I have had a longstanding love of international cinema, including Japanese cinema and, since first seeing his films, I have thought of Ozu as my favorite filmmaker. But when it comes to Chinese films, I am once again playing catch-up and for a similar reason as with early cinema. Until I met Richie, my exposure to Chinese cinema had been predictable: I had seen and loved John Woo's Hong Kong films and Zhang Yimou's astonishingly beautiful work, and those films still stand for me the best of contemporary world cinema. But *The Peach Girl, The Goddess,* and *Wild Rose*? Never heard of them. Jin Yan, Ruan Lingyu, Wang Renmei? Never heard of them. Richie Meyer has literally opened new doors to Chinese cinema for me and for many Westerners with his important books about these three actors and DVD productions of these three films.

With this book Meyer once again brings attention to a comparatively obscure actress in the English-speaking world and to a film that few have seen. Important as this is, his work is distinguished by much more. Meyer always places his subject within a precise historical, cultural, and film production context. This book provocatively examines the paradox of Renmei's promising career as a star from the mid-1930s, which never materialized after a brilliant start. Meyer places this career trajectory within the context of antifeminist, feudal traditions in China as well as the fate of many leftists from Shanghai of that generation. He also carefully traces Renmei's life; her rise to stardom in *Wild Rose*; her marriage to her co-star, Jin Yan, leading to the studio not renewing her contract in the belief that a married woman would not appeal to the male audience; and later her second marriage to the artist Ye Qianyu, as well as her mental breakdowns and physical health problems.

Meyer always writes in an accessible, jargon-free style that invites all interested readers to share his enthusiasm and knowledge for the films he loves so much within their richest historical, cultural, and biographical contexts. Thanks to this wonderful book, the name Wang Renmei and the film *Wild Rose* will no longer be obscure within the English-speaking world of film scholarship. As coincidence would have it, I write this introduction at a time in my life when China is of increasing importance to me personally, as it is to many Westerners. Last year I had the opportunity to visit China and spent a week at Sichuan University, giving a couple of lectures on American cinema and participating in the Center for American Culture. On the way back, I had a brief stay in Beijing where I met Professor Lui Zhaohui and her family. This year Professor Lui, from North China Electric Power University, is a visiting research fellow in the Center for Film, Media and Popular Culture at Arizona State University. We meet weekly, not just to talk about movies, but to learn about each other's culture. I conclude on this personal note because, thanks to Meyer and his wonderful scholarship on Chinese film of which this book is the latest installment, I already have some historical and cultural context for understanding the cinema from a country that is becoming increasingly important in my life. I thank him for that and I think you will too, in whatever context you read this book. You will enjoy it, learn from it, and be enriched by it.

I will never catch up with Richie (he is in New Zealand as I write this), but it sure is fun trying.

Peter Lehman
Director of the Center for Film, Media and Popular Culture
Arizona State University
Tempe
January 2012

Preface

Although I write about the life and work of Wang Renmei, it has to be noted that her life was intertwined with Mao Zedong, one of the most influential Chinese leaders of the twentieth century. Her family was early supporters and followers of the man who led the Communist Party of China (CCP) for over 40 years. Not only that, their early years were deeply interwoven and in many ways Wang can be seen as the embodiment of Mao's early ideals about women, athleticism, and the youth of China.

As a young man, Mao was a close friend of Wang's father and lived in his house, during which time he and Renmei saw each other on a daily basis. Later, as director of the school she attended, he disseminated to her ideas that young people, particularly women, should become physically fit in order to save the fate of China. This was a lesson she took to heart and it defined her identity as a film star. Wang remained a believer in the ideals of Mao's early years, but after the Long March, when he began a period of austere and doctrinaire policies in the caves of Yan'an, she made a decision not to join him there. She was too comfortable in Shanghai. Wang lost contact with the chairman at that time. Later, in Mao's old age, he repeatedly asked for her, even though she had been passed over several times for membership in the CCP.

Even after Wang had become an internationally recognized actress, the movie star still held fast to the teaching she had learned from Mao while he was in charge of her school. It is for this reason, I felt it important to cover aspects of his life so that the reader unfamiliar with Mao's early life and philosophy can understand the umbrella-like context they formed for the movie star. In the same way, by understanding Wang's life and decisions as an artist, we can see even more clearly how Mao's later ideals deviated from the essence of his original, youthful idealism, which persisted in Wang.

As mentioned, Wang Renmei was influenced by Mao in several ways. She agreed with his desire to revolutionize China by transforming herself. Her commitment to strength and athleticism began during her school days when the later chairman was head of Wang's school. She and Mao also believed that they showed the same Hunan characteristics of toughness and contrasts. Members of her household worked for him and were influenced by his ideals as well.

For many reasons, I have included the plot summaries of all of the films in which Wang appeared, however small her part. Jin Yan, the most famous male superstar of the 1930s and Wang's first husband, believed that Chinese movies at that time could not be separated from the actual issues of China. Their plots not only showed the *Zeitgeist* of the times but the veiled attacks on the social system and the government leveled by the artists who actually witnessed the events that were destroying their country. Another reason is that during my many visits to the China Film Archive in Beijing, I discovered that many of Wang Renmei's films are inaccessible. The plots need to be known in English for the first time, not only as research material for future scholars and students interested in her films (the main object for whom this book is written), but also because they were part of the folklore that developed as China unfolded a response to its disastrous period.

Wang Renmei's biography could have been a screenplay. Although she became a famous film star and was healthy and athletic, she fell ill to depression and mental ailments. Her two marriages were unfulfilled. The first one was responsible for her losing her job at a film studio. The second one resulted in loneliness. She once remarked that marriage was often the tomb of a woman's career. Wang faced hardships during World War II, as did China. Her rich life turned into one of survival. She was forced to flee Hong Kong to become a housekeeper and typist, but after the conflagration, her pluckiness enabled her to return to movie making and accept any role no matter how small. When she could not get acting jobs, she worked making costumes for studio productions and carried out continuity assignments. Wang became sick during the Cultural Revolution but did not suffer the fate of her fellow artists because of her ties to Mao. Her life reflected the social history of China during its turbulent period in the twentieth century. In many ways, one might almost argue that she was the forgotten daughter of Mao, the daughter born from his early commitment to women's rights and physical education and then forgotten in the horror of his mass campaigns.

Introduction

I first saw the film *Wild Rose* in Pordenone at the world's largest silent film festival. There, with screenings of other films from the Golden Age of Chinese Films, I discovered this masterpiece film from the Hollywood of Asia. Over the next decade and a half, I proceeded to seek out and view, in depth, those magnificent motion pictures, mostly at the China Film Archive in Beijing. In addition, I started to research the lives of many of the stars who made this period so famous.

Thanks to my son, Mahlon, who is fluent in Mandarin and a writer and teacher himself, I was able to access and understand the materials about this period and the actors who appeared on the screen.

My first book about Ruan Lingyu, the brilliant actress who took her own life at the age of 24 at the height of her career, led me to her co-star Jin Yan. After finishing his biography, I realized that no history of Chinese film would be complete without a book about Wang Renmei, Jin's first wife who was a marvelous singer and screen star at an early age. Too early, it seemed as I unfolded her history — a history also affected by Chairman Mao Zedong.

All of these actors played in films which reflect the turbulent times of China in the twentieth century. Both Jin and Wang experienced the Japanese invasion, World War II, the Chinese Civil War, the creation of the People's Republic of China and the Cultural Revolution. Their careers and lives were affected by all of these events.

I am grateful to the hardworking staff of the China Film Archive in Beijing for making materials and films available to me. Several people in China spent time with me to talk about their experiences and their knowledge of Wang Renmei. I want to thank Qin Yi, Wang Yong, and Yuhua Dong especially. Assisting me with translation, in addition to Mahlon, were Yong Wei and Xinyu Dong.

I have used the pinyin system of romanization in the text except for the well-known names and historical references.

My wife Susan Harmon encouraged me to write another book. She, together with Michelle Cash, helped with typing the text and Michelle and Nona Perry assisted with transcriptions. Dr. Edwin Weihe, chairman of film studies at Seattle University, supported my efforts.

Finally, I would like to thank Michael Duckworth, publisher of Hong Kong University Press, and his talented staff, for giving me yet another opportunity to tell the story of Shanghai film stars with this book about "Wildcat" Wang Renmei.

Richard J. Meyer
Wellington, New Zealand
March 2013

Cast of Characters in the Life of Wang Renmei

In order of appearance in the text

Mao Zedong – chairman of the Communist Party of China 1945–1976; chairman of the People's Republic of China 1954–1959.

Wang Zhengshu (Li'an) – father of Wang Renmei, teacher of Mao Zedong.

Wang "Xixi" – youngest daughter of Wang Zhengshu; her name was later changed to Wang Renmei.

Dr. Sun Yat-sen – played a role in the overthrow of the Qing dynasty in 1911; first provisional president of the Republic of China in 1912; co-founded Guomindang.

Yuan Shikai – second provisional president of the Republic of China 1912–1915; self-proclaimed emperor of China 1915–1916.

Chiang Kai-shek – president of the Republic of China 1948–1949; president of the Republic of China on Taiwan 1950–1975; leader of Guomindang.

Wang Renxuan – Wang Renmei's oldest brother.

Zhu De – commander-in-chief of the People's Liberation Army, 1946–1954.

Li Jinhui – founder and director of the Bright Moon Troupe; director of the Meimei School; father of Chinese popular music.

Wang Renda – brother of Wang Renmei.

Wang Renlu – brother of Wang Renmei.

Wang Renyi – brother of Wang Renmei.

Li Minghui – Classmate of Wang Renmei at Meimei School; fellow performer and singer with the Bright Moon Troupe; Shanghai movie star.

Luo Mingyou – owner and operator of movie theaters all over China in the 1920s and founder of Lianhua Studios.

Sun Yu – U.S. trained director who worked at Min Xin and Lianhua.

Shi Dongshan – one of China's leading directors from the 1920s to 1950s.

Li Ming – caretaker of Wang Renmei in 1929, stage performer; underground member of the Chinese Communist Party.

Jin Yan – considered to be the most popular male movie star in Shanghai in the 1930s; first husband of Wang Renmei.

Situ Huimin – pioneer of Chinese sound reproduction.

Cai Chusheng – film director at Lianhua Studios.

Tian Han – famous Communist writer.

Nie Er – composer of many leftist songs, as well as the official anthem of the People's Republic of China.

Zhang Shankun – flamboyant impresario and film producer; director of Xinhua Film Company.

Wu Yonggang – well-known director whose first film, *The Goddess,* is considered to be one of the top ten films made in China.

Tian Fang – head of the Beijing Film Studio and vice-dean of the Central Movie Bureau.

Ye Qianyu – well-known Chinese painter and second husband of Wang Renmei.

Qin Yi – second wife of Jin Yan; famous actress of Chinese films and friend of Wang Renmei.

Madame Mao (Jiang Qing) – actress in Chinese films during the 1930s; married Mao Zedong in Yan'an in 1940; one of the Gang of Four.

Deng Xiaoping – paramount leader of the People's Republic of China from 1978 to 1992.

Yuhua Dong – student leader during the Cultural Revolution.

Dr. Wang Yong – professor at Shanghai Conservatory of Music and noted author.

Photo 1.1 Mao Zedong was a student of Wang Renmei's father and stayed at her home one summer.

Photo 1.2 Wang Renmei (taken in 1929 in Shenyang).

Photo 1.3 Wang Renmei in the center in *Three Butterflies* (1930). She played a flower in the Bright Moon Troupe's tour of southeast Asia.

Photo 1.4 Wang Renmei, on the right, in her performance in *Peach Plum Strive in the Spring* for the Bright Moon Troupe.

Photo 1.5 American-trained Sun Yu discovered Wang Renmei when she appeared with the Bright Moon Troupe. He was known as the "poet director."

Photo 1.6 Wang Renmei as she was discovered by director Sun Yu.

Photo 1.7 Wang Renmei, as a member of the Bright Moon Troupe, participated in the film *Poetry on Palm Leaves*. It was a failure and had an unsuccessful soundtrack.

Photo 1.8 Li Jinhui, founder and director of the Bright Moon Troupe; director of the Meimei School; father of Chinese popular music.

Photo 1.9 Director Cai Chusheng worked with Wang Renmei on *The Spring Tide*, which was a box office flop. He vowed to make a better film with her and did with the successful *The Morning of a Metropolis*.

Photo 1.10 Wang Renmei was the first Chinese actress to show bare legs in the film *Wild Rose*.

Photo 1.11 *Wild Rose* made Wang Renmei famous. She played Xiao Feng, with Lianhua favorite Zhang Zhizhi as her father.

Photo 1.12 Wang Renmei got the nickname "Wildcat" for her active enthusiasm in films.

Photo 1.13 Jin Yan, Wang Renmei's first husband, taught her to ride horses in the suburbs of Shanghai. This skill helped her to mount the animal in later films.

Photo 1.14 Wang Renmei, in the film *The Morning of a Metropolis,* plays Xu Lan'er, who visits her brother Qiling in jail.

Photo 1.15 Wang Renmei as Lan'er and Gao Zhanfei as Qiling in *The Morning of a Metropolis*, directed by Cai Chusheng.

Photo 1.16 The production team of *The Morning of a Metropolis*. Front row from the right: Meng Junmou, Cai Chusheng, Zhou Ke, Han Langen.

Photo 1.17 Wang Renmei in *Song of the Fishermen* as Little Cat with her brother Little Monkey, played by Han Langen. The title song, written by Nie Er, increased Wang's popularity with her recording of the lyrics.

Photo 1.18 Wang Renmei sings "Song of the Fishermen" while her brother helps with the net. He dies at the end of the film and asks his sister to sing it one more time.

Photo 1.19 Wang Renmei with the cast on location in the tiny village of Shipu where they filmed *Song of the Fishermen*. The director could only find a small fishing boat for the shoot which caused many actors to become seasick.

Photo 1.20 Nie Er, famous Chinese composer who wrote the music for *Song of the Fishermen* and other films; his song "March of the Volunteers" became China's national anthem.

Photo 1.21 *Song of the Fishermen* with Wang Renmei as Little Cat, Han Langen as Little Monkey, and Pei Yiwei as the uncle.

Photo 1.22 Wang Renmei as Yan Yuying in the play, *The Song for Returning Spring*. Music was written by Nie Er, with script by Tian Han.

Photo 1.23 Wang Renmei as Ma Nina and Mei Xi as Zhu Dongxin in *The Song of Perpetual Regret*. This was her first film for the newly created Xinhua Enterprises, established by Zhang Shankun.

Photo 1.24 Wu Yonggang became famous when his first film *The Goddess* was considered a masterpiece. He directed Wang Renmei in three films for Xinhua Enterprises, including *Soaring Aspirations*, *Pirates of the Yellow Sea*, and *Parting from Heaven with Sorrow*.

Photo 1.25 Wang Renmei in *Soaring Aspirations* is reunited with her husband Jin Yan in a story about villagers who rise up and fight back many times against countless attacks by bandits. The villains represent the Japanese.

Photo 1.26 Wang Renmei plays Black Clown, who is killed at the end of *Soaring Aspirations*. Her death inspires the villagers to fight to the bitter end.

Photo 1.27 Wang Renmei with Jin Yan, who plays Shun'er in *Soaring Aspirations*. He shouts, "If we retreat, where would we go? This is our land."

Photo 1.28 Wang Renmei plays Ah Feng, a singsong girl, in *Sons and Daughters of Wind and Cloud*. She sings Nie Er's song, "The Singsong Girls Under the Iron Hoof," which inserted a note of patriotic urgency into the film.

Photo 1.29 Wang Renmei performing on stage in *Sons and Daughters of Wind and Cloud*. The script was written by Communist Tian Han who was hiding from the Guomindang secret police.

Photo 1.30 After the end of World War II, Wang Renmei was thrilled with the opportunity to resume her career and star in the film *Boundless Spring*.

Photo 1.31 Wang and her husband, played by Zhao Dan, in *Boundless Spring*. She leaves him at the end of the film to start a new life on a farm.

Photo 1.32 Wang Renmei, third row center in front of the camera, poses with the cast and crew of *The Story of Visiting Family*. She plays a young village girl in flashback scenes.

Photo 1.33 After a successful performance in the play *Family*, Wang Renmei was given an opportunity to play a humiliated spouse abandoned by her husband in *The Steps of Youth*.

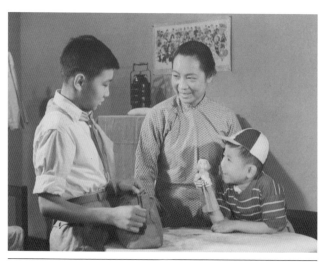

Photo 1.34 Wang Renmei plays a small part as the friend of the lead actor's mother. The film *Flowers* tells the story of children who form a group to celebrate various holidays.

Photo 1.35 Wang Renmei and Japanese film actress
Sugimura Haruko in Beijing, May, 1956.

Photo 1.36 Jiang Qing (Madame Mao), wife of
Chairman Mao Zedong and former Shanghai film
actress, on trial as a member of the Gang of Four.

Photo 1.37 Qin Yi, famous Chinese actress; second wife of Jin Yan and friend of Wang Renmei.

Photo 1.38 Mao led the Communists on the Long March to Yan'an where he had his headquarters. Wang Renmei regretted not going there to join him but her life in Shanghai was too comfortable.

Photo 1.39 Chiang Kai-shek, president of the Republic of China, 1948–1949; president of the Republic of China on Taiwan, 1950–1975; leader of Guomindang.

Photo 1.40 Zhou Enlai, premier of the People's Republic of China; defender of the film industry and other arts during the Cultural Revolution.

Photo 1.41 Deng Xiaoping, paramount leader of the People's Republic of China, 1978–1992.

Photo 1.42 One of many caricatures of Wang Renmei from the tabloid Shanghai press of the 1930s; she usually found them to be funny and laughed them off.

Photo 1.43 Ye Qianyu, second husband of Wang Renmei and successful painter and teacher; he had drawn a caricature of Wang years before they met, she was amused at the time.

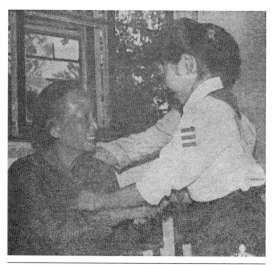

Photo 1.44 Wang Renmei with the schoolchildren of the Wang Fujing Primary School, 1981.

CHAPTER 1

Land of Fish and Rice

. . . crowded years and months of endeavor,
Young we were, and schoolmates,
In high assurance, fearless
Pointing the finger at all things . . .
Under the unmoving sky a million creatures try out their
freedom
I ponder, I ask the boundless earth,
Who rules over destiny?
Do you remember?
How, reaching midstream, we struck the waters,
And the waves dashed against our speeding boats?[1]

The poem, "Changsha," written by Mao Zedong about his days at the First Normal School in Changsha was a poem of nostalgia. He remembered the experience that he had under the leadership of math teacher Wang Zhengshu (Li'an) at the First Normal School in Hunan.

The future leader of the world's most populous nation spent many happy days at the home of teacher Wang during the turbulent years after the overthrow of the Qing dynasty in 1911. In fact, one summer he spent the entire vacation living at the educator's home. During that time, he had an opportunity to get acquainted with the entire Wang family, including the ten children and other relatives who stayed with the family.

It was a happy time for the teenage Mao, even though he was beginning to see the injustices of the contemporary Chinese society.

The young student was particularly fond of the youngest daughter of teacher Wang whose nickname was "Xixi," which meant double slight or thin. She later took the name of "Wang Renmei" when she was older. Renmei remembers that she would sit bouncing on the knee of this young student and never contemplated what the future would hold.

What Mao discovered living with the Wang family was a typical feudalistic family with modern ideas. For example, none of the daughters had their feet bound, nor did the female servants. Wang Zhengshu was not only a famous mathematics teacher in the province, he also tutored his children and others in classical Chinese, calligraphy, and medicine. He collected rare books which Mao had the opportunity to read. At the dinner table, children were expected to discuss the great Confucius classics that they had read. Even the servants were asked to recite. No one laughed at the poorly educated servant who made amusing mistakes when reading these texts, but the kindly teacher believed that a classical education was the foundation of the future of a modern China. He believed that learning could rescue the country from foreign imperialists and industrial development would make the nation stronger. He encouraged his children to study abroad.[2]

Mao, as a student at the First Normal School, was free and easy when he spoke, never getting flustered, losing his temper, or speaking in anger. However, when it came to the feudal autocratic work style, he was not as temperate. In his views, "he made absolutely no compromise."[3]

Each day, as Mao walked to school, he experienced firsthand the corruption of the ruling class. He "had a deep hatred for the entire old feudal order. He despised the gentry, whose mouths were full of benevolence and righteousness, for their meanness and their falseness . . ."[4]

As the First Normal School was located alongside the railroad, Mao observed that whenever troops came and invaded by train, the school was the first target. Sometimes the soldiers took everything in sight, including food and firewood. Other times, the students would not permit the soldiers to enter and so the troops simply took over the large dormitory. The young student was a witness to the killings and theft of the various warlords' men.[5]

Mao's grades in math were poor because he was more interested in other subjects and reading his own books. Despite this, Wang Renmei's father, the math teacher, still had a high regard for Mao because of his abilities as a natural leader in the school. Her father was instrumental in preventing Mao from being expelled from the First Normal School in an incident in which the young student stirred the student union to fight red tape. Mao harassed the stuffy and corrupt principal whom Mao called "Mr. Turn-back-the-clock." He also was one of the leaders persuading students to barricade the school against soldiers who wanted to loot.[6]

Several authors hint that the province of Hunan ("south of the lake") and the capital city of Changsha ("long sands"), known as the "land of fish and rice," were an influence not only on Mao but on many people who came from that province and contributed to the development of the Chinese nation. The attributes of Hunanese people can be summed up with the quote in Ross Terrill's biography of Mao, "China can be concurred only when every Hunanese is dead," these people "fight and curse and state their views with gusto." Terrill says that they are known as China's Prussians.[7]

Other writers claim the ancient beauty of Hunan Province was instrumental in the development of its people. Hunan is a temperate region with misty undulating hills that have been populated ever since the Neolithic Age. Buddhist temples dating from the Tang dynasty (AD 618–906), when Buddhism first came here, are still in use. Three hundred species of trees grow in the hills where wild animals still roamed in the early twentieth century. Bertrand Russell, who visited in 1921, viewed Changsha just like a medieval town with narrow streets and no traffic possible except sedan chairs and rickshaws. The First Normal School, where Professor Wang taught and Mao studied, was built in a Romanesque style with a wide column porch. The classrooms had wooden floors and glass windows.[8]

Hunan was a land of contrasts as Wang Renmei and Mao Zedong grew up—contrast between the natural environment and the marauding soldiers; contrast between old feudalistic ideas and the emerging revolutionary movements started by Dr. Sun Yat-sen and which challenged the ancient dynasties which had ruled China for thousands of years.

Three years before Wang Renmei was born in 1914, the old Manchu dynasty was overthrown. In Changsha, as in most areas of China, people rose up against the soldiers of the Qing dynasty. However, Mao observed that the leaders of the rebellion were killed in the street and the representatives of the gentry took over. He really believed that they were killed because they were poor and stood for the interests of the oppressed and that the landlords and merchants were dissatisfied with them. This led Mao to join the revolutionary forces where he spent most of his six months in the army reading newspapers.

On New Year's Day 1912, Dr. Sun Yat-sen was sworn in at Nanjing as China's first president. Yuan Shikai, who became the next provisional president, was about to challenge Sun's leadership and the Hunanese were preparing to oppose him. Sun and Yuan came to an agreement and on February 12, the emperor abdicated. Two days later, Sun stepped down in Yuan's favor. A few months later, Mao decided to return to school.

The province of Hunan was caught up in the struggle between Sun and Yuan from 1912 to 1916. During this time, the reformist governor was ousted by Yuan and the Changsha arsenal was blown up. Yuan proclaimed himself emperor in 1915 and capitulated to Japan, which was when secret societies rebelled against Beijing's appointed governor of Hunan. These efforts failed, but the governor declared Hunan independent. That government fell in 1916 after the governor fled and Yuan died. Prolonged political chaos followed with weeks of bloodletting and internal strife in Changsha.

During all those years of turbulence, Wang Renmei's father continued to instruct Mao and other students at the First Normal School, even though for many months teachers went unpaid. Many students fled, but Mao remained and received his teaching diploma in June of 1918 when Renmei was four years old.[9]

Mao considered the time when he returned to the First Normal School, after his brief army service as one of the most influential periods of his life. He developed his mind, writing ability, and physical strength. In 1915, he was elected secretary of the Students' Society at the First Normal school and two years later, he had a leading role in forming the New People's Study Society, Xinmin Xuehui, which was one of the most radical student groups in China at that time. "Virtually its entire membership ultimately joined the Communist Party." Mao graduated from the First Normal School in spring 1918 and returned to Hunan in the summer of 1919 after a half of a year in Beijing where he had participated in the political activity that followed the May Fourth student demonstrations. According to Stuart Schram, "he had already set his foot on the path that would lead him shortly to a career as a professional Revolutionary." Mao became director of the primary school that was attached to the First Normal School in 1920 and subsequently became a Marxist. Attending the primary school was little Wang Renmei, whose path seemed to be intertwined with that of the new primary school director.[10]

In his work at the school, Mao continued to follow what he had written in 1917 in "a study of physical culture," which was published in *Hsin Ch'ing-nien* (New Youth) in 1917. He wrote:

> Our nation is wanting in strength. The military spirit has not been encouraged. The physical condition of the population deteriorates daily. This is an extremely disturbing phenomena . . . If this state continues, our weakness will increase further. To attain our goals and make our influence felt are external matters, results. The development of our physical strength is an internal matter, a cause. If our bodies are not strong, we will be afraid as soon as we see enemy soldiers, and then how can we attain our goals and make ourselves respected? . . . The principle aim of physical education is military heroism.[11]

Mao's emphasis on physical education influenced young Wang Renmei when she entered the primary school at age six. "I did not feel the curriculum was very difficult because I already studied classical Chinese and mathematics at home and two of my sisters were teachers. So, I did not want to spend too much time in studying—I really liked sports."[12]

Notes

1. Ross Terrill, *A Biography: Mao* (New York: Harper and Row Publishers, 1980), p. 76.
2. Wang Renmei, *Memoir: Wo de chengming yu buxing,* Xie Bo (ed.) (Shanghai: Shanghai Art Press [Shanghai: Wenyi Chubanshe], 1985), pp. 3–6.
3. Li Jui, *The Early Revolutionary Activities of Comrade Mao Tse-Tung*, Anthony W. Sariti (trans.), James C. Hsiung (ed.) (White Plains, NY: M.E. Sharpe 1977), pp. 43–44.
4. Li, *The Early Revolutionary Activities of Comrade Mao Tse-Tung*, p. 46.
5. Ibid., pp. 46–49.
6. Terrill, *A Biography: Mao*, p. 32.
7. Ibid., pp. 6–7.
8. Jung Chang and Jon Halliday, *Mao: The Unknown Story* (New York: Alfred A. Knopf, 2005), pp. 2–11.
9. Phillip Short, *Mao: A Life* (New York: Henry Holt & Company, LLC., 1999), pp. 46–78.
10. Stuart Schram, *Mao Tse-tung* (New York: Simon and Schuster, second printing, 1966), pp. 38–51.
11. Ibid., pp. 28–36.
12. Wang Renmei, *Memoir: Wo de chengming yu buxing*, p. 20.

CHAPTER 2

The Bright Moon Troupe

Dressed in a crisp new school uniform with a gray shirt and a black skirt, 12-year-old Wang Renmei looked forward to her first year at the Hunan Provincial First Female Normal School. She aspired to do better in mathematics because of the influence of her father. She learned *Guoyu*, the standard oral Chinese used nationwide similar to Putonghua, but still used the Hunan dialect while doing the mathematical calculations subconsciously. She also spent a lot of time climbing Mount Yuelu in Changsha and was very active physically, but for the most part she neglected her studies and dropped out after her first year. She believed that this limitation in her education became an obstacle in her later career in movies. She also believed that it was a reason for her mental problems.[1]

Around the same time as she left the Normal School, her father died at the age of 60. Renmei's brothers and sisters returned home from different parts of China to attend the funeral. Her second oldest brother, who returned from Shanghai, drew a portrait of their father for the funeral party. Her third oldest brother decided to open a portrait drawing shop in Changsha and asked Renmei to serve as a receptionist after school. Portrait drawing was a popular way of reproducing the likeness of an individual because copying photographs, at that time, was still expensive. Fortunately for the young pre-teenager, her siblings continued to fund her education. At the time when the funeral was held, China was again beset by internal strife. The Northern Expedition to reunify China began in July of 1926. In Hunan, the local commander staged a successful rebellion and was backed by Chiang Kai-shek. At the same time, Mao was advising the Guomindang about getting peasant support in the campaign. He was appointed the secretary of the Communist Party's (CCP) Peasant Movement Committee in Shanghai in November and his wife and children returned to Hunan. The combined forces of the Communist Party under the Guomindang successfully defeated the warlords in the north and when the Northern army returned to Shanghai in April 1927, members of the Communist Party in Shanghai were massacred by the Guomindang and the Green Gang. The violence spread to Hunan where 10,000 people in Changsha alone were killed as suspected Communists. Overall, 300,000 people perished all over the province and Mao was appointed to coordinate the affairs in the province as the Communist Party's Hunan party secretary.[2]

The Wang family fled Changsha at that time and gathered in Wuhan. Wang Renmei recalled the huge celebrations in Wuhan celebrating the so-called victory of the Northern Expedition. Wang Renmei's oldest brother, Wang Renxuan, was sent to Germany to purchase ammunition for the new government. While in Germany, her brother met Zhu De, a senior member of the Communist Party and one of the founders of the People's Liberation Army (PLA), and immediately joined the Chinese Communist Party. He was impressed by Zhu De. Renxuan returned to Wuhan after studying in the Soviet Union and became a member of the Ad Hoc Executive Committee of Guomindang, which was pro-Communist. That group worked against Chiang Kai-shek. Other members of Wang Renmei's family got involved with the Communist Party, including her stepmother, Cao Yi'er. During the Northern Expedition, Cao was responsible for the family affairs of Mao Zedong. Mao was fond of her son, Wang Jineng, and called him "Mao Mao." Cao later became a spy for the Communist Party there. She was killed after a raid by the Japanese air force in 1938 and her son Jineng was adopted by a cousin and later sent to Renmei's oldest brother. He became an engineer when he grew up.[3]

In late 1927, the Wang family fled Wuhan for Wuxi. In early 1928, Wang Renmei's second oldest brother decided to send her and her third oldest brother to the Meimei School in Shanghai. The Meimei School was not an ordinary school. It was a transition between the Zhongguo Gewu Special School for Singing and Dancing and the Zhongguo Singing and Dancing Troupe. The Meimei School was free and even provided room and board for the students who learned singing and dancing. The brother was assigned to the band section to learn how to play the mandolin, since he already had knowledge of the violin. Wang Renmei was sent to the singing and dancing class. The Meimei School was started by Li Jinhui, the former editor and chief of *Xiaopengyou*. The curriculum of Wang Renmei's new school was rigorous. Only 40 students were admitted to the facility, which consisted of young girls and boys aged 15 to 18. There were six classes each day: four of the classes were singing and dancing class; two of them were so-called culture class. The culture classes consisted of current political events, foreign languages, theater knowledge, and music theory. The singing and dancing classes focused on singing, playing musical instruments, performing, and dancing. The textbooks used were edited by Li Jinhui, who taught his own songs and choreography.

After three months of study, students had to demonstrate what they had learned in a special singing and dancing show. The faculty at the Meimei School included Li Jinhui, who taught music, and a dancing teacher named Wei Yingbo. Older students served as mentors for the younger ones, including Li Jinhui's daughter Li Minghui. All of the students lived and studied together and considered themselves sisters and brothers. The older students used the national language when they sang. However, in daily conversation, they used either the Shanghai dialect or the Ningbo dialect. They spoke very fast and since Renmei only spoke the Hunan dialect, she could not understand the older students when they spoke to her and they did not understand what she repeated back to them. Finally, she learned the Shanghai dialect and became very happy at the school.

After a few weeks at the Meimei School, Director Li had all of the students and faculty move to his home in the foreign concessions because there was more room. Wang Renmei seldom had contact with the director because he locked himself in his room, focusing on writing new songs for a tour he was contemplating. He wanted to take the students to southeast Asia where they could perform before the Chinese communities in that part of the continent. When Renmei became more acquainted with Mr. Li, he suggested that she change her given name to the one that she is now known by. He said, "Why is it that a female offspring cannot have the generation name?" At that time, the feudal system stated that only boys could have the generation name, which was "Ren." The director believed that males and females should be equal and therefore should have their generation name in their character. (The Wang brothers all have the "Ren" character in their names: Wang Renda, Wang Renxuan, Wang Renlu, and Wang Renyi.)

Teenager Wang Renmei learned children's singing and dancing. The songs were written by Mr. Li and enabled her to develop a style of singing that would later make her famous. She performed three songs that were representative of compositions by Li Jinhui: "Poor Qiuxing," "Sparrow and Child," and "Little Painter." The songs combined singing and dancing. The idea of the singing and dancing show, which combined music and dancing, was to teach children the value of honesty and integrity. Many of the students who performed at the Meimei School later went on to careers in the motion picture industry in Shanghai. Li Minghui was a well-known film star in the 1930s.

After a year of rehearsals, the first Zhongguo Singing and Dancing Troupe was organized to tour southeast Asia. The ten-month trip gave Wang Renmei the experience of performing before varied audiences. Li Jinhui's troupe said goodbye to the Meimei School, which closed after their departure, and visited Hangzhou and Ningbo as rehearsal for the overseas tour. The troupe to southeast Asia had 30 members, including Renmei's brother, Renlu, who was made stage manager. The company visited Singapore, Hong Kong, Jakarta, and other cities with large populations of overseas Chinese. Wherever they went, the group was received warmly. In addition to entertaining Chinese audiences, they used the national Chinese language and spread propaganda for the Communist Party. At age 14, Wang Renmei experienced life as a traveling performer involved in political activity.

The show was impressive. One of the songs performed was the memorial song to President Sun Yat-sen. It was performed by ten girls in white skirts in two lines when the lyrics were heard by the audience, "Our President first launched the revolution . . . the blood of revolution was red as flower . . . he toppled down despotism and established Zhongguo." In Hong Kong, Wang remembered, the audience stood up to show their respect to Sun Yat-sen. The British audience in Hong Kong stood up as well, but reluctantly. The overseas Chinese welcomed the troupe and praised them for bringing honor to China. They said it was the very first time in colonial Hong Kong when Chinese people sang a song that the British had to stand up for. The show was basically the same in each performance. It had five parts, including singing, dancing, and drama. The drama also had singing and dancing.

In Jakarta, the Dutch colonial government censored the performance of the memorial song to Sun Yat-sen, but the local overseas Chinese asked them to give more performances, which they did not advertise in advance. The regional Chinese conveyed the message orally that the performances were to be given; the tickets were sold out and the song was sung. It demonstrated to Wang Renmei how organized the overseas Chinese were.

Although Wang Renmei, during her time at the Meimei School, was able to perform various songs as a soloist, when she went on the tour to southeast Asia, all of her parts were secondary, or as she put it, "back-up parts." She played a flower in the play, *Three Butterflies,* and the beetle in *Grape Fairy*. She had her opportunity for stardom in one of the performances when the lead singer, Li Minghui, became mute and the show *Little Painter* had already started. The cast was nervous. Wang Renmei suggested that Minghui act on the stage and she, singing backstage, could perform for Minghui. Minghui lip-synched the singing as Renmei belted out the lyrics. The dubbing experience would be useful for Wang Renmei when she made her first sound film in her later career. The audience discovered that she had sung for the performer and found it to be quite exciting. Her salary was doubled from two to four yuan.

At the beginning of 1929, the troupe returned to China and was dismissed. Wang Renmei did not have any idea of where to go. Her second oldest brother asked Li Ming, a member of the Communist Party, to take care of her, as they were classmates in Germany. Li Ming sent her to a school to study English but she discovered it was much too difficult and dropped out of the English school. Her caretaker, Li Ming, rented a piano so that Wang Renmei could sing and play in exchange for going back to the school. She agreed and every day after school she would sit down in front of the piano and practice her various songs. She recalled that many people would come to the window and listen to her play, but her study of English was not satisfactory. In order to pass the examination, she just memorized the whole chapter. As a performer, however, her pronunciation was excellent. The head of the school, hearing her recite, asked her to sing English songs or recite some poetry. At the age of 15, she suddenly discovered that she could perform in front of an audience in a foreign language and memorize the lyrics perfectly. The audience was thrilled and that experience helped her become the leading actress for the Bright Moon Troupe shortly afterwards. Director Li of the school was so impressed with her that he hired Wang Renmei to teach singing and dancing to the other students. She later remarked, "Only several months after I entered the school, I had become a teacher from a student."[4]

In the winter of 1929, Li Jinhui established the Bright Moon Troupe and asked Wang Renmei, along with some of her fellow students from the school, including her brother Wang Renyi, to join the troupe. They rehearsed every day and developed quite a repertoire of songs. Wang Renmei became the lead singer. In the spring of 1930, the Bright Moon Troupe moved to Beijing. Its first performance was at Tsinghua University. The play *Three Butterflies* was performed.

Renmei played the part of a red butterfly. The show was so successful that other universities asked the Bright Moon Troupe to perform. Wherever they appeared, the tickets were sold out within hours after going on sale. They toured Tianjin, Harbin, and other cities in northeast China.

The following year in early 1931, Luo Mingyou, the director of Lianhua Motion Picture Studios, heard about the Bright Moon Troupe. He recruited the entire group into the movie company and its name was changed to the Lianhua Singing and Dancing Troupe. Several short movies of singing and dancing were made that were supposed to be incorporated into the film called *Yinhe Shuangxing* (*Double Stars Shining in the Milky Way*, a.k.a. *Two Stars Shining in the Milky Way*). *Double Stars Shining in the Milky Way* involved the entire company of the Lianhua Studios. It was on the set that Wang Renmei was discovered by Director Sun Yu. The star of the film, Jin Yan, had been discovered by Sun Yu earlier. At that time, he was becoming the most famous male star of Chinese films.[5]

Wang Renmei and the Lianhua Singing and Dancing Troupe shot several short excerpts of singing and dancing, most of which were never put into the film because of the problems with the soundtrack. The short scenes of singing and dancing without sound were integrated into the film. One can see segments from the skits, *The Night of the Wedding* and *Butterfly Girls,* without sound. The other segments, including, *Women Army, Blowing Bubbles, Song of the Dancing Partner*, and *Small Song Thrushbird,* were never seen again because of technical difficulties. Director Shi Dongshan involved the entire company of actors as well as directors and crew of the Lianhua Studios. The project was a chance for the company to showcase its many performers. This was not unlike special films made by Hollywood studios in the 1930s and 1940s which were used as promotional motion pictures to publicize the actors.

The plot of *Double Stars Shining in the Milky Way* involves a young girl, Li Yueying, who loves to sing and is very good. She and her father live as hermits in a remote hamlet. The old man was originally a prolific songwriter in southeast Asia and had taught his daughter how to sing. One spring, the Double Star Film Company is shooting a film in the area and the director is captivated by the girl and resolves to make her a star in a sound film. He invites the company's management to the small town. The manager observes the girl's talent at singing and dancing and personally asks the girl to play a role in the historical drama, *The Bitter Palace*. In her first appearance, Li plays opposite the lead part of the Tang dynasty emperor, Xuanzong, played by Liu Qian. Liu, played by rising star Jin Yan, falls in love with the young girl. Her father hopes that the love affair will end in marriage, but unfortunately, Liu already has a wife. He hides his grief each time he sees Li. Soon, he begins to avoid her. She pines for him, not knowing the reason for his distance.

After a few months, the filming of the *Bitter Palace* is complete. The film company holds a banquet for all members of the cast and crew. During the banquet, Li's love is reignited as she and Liu dance the tango. The conscience of the actor starts to bother him and he realizes that he cannot consummate his relationship with the girl and leaves. A month later he returns, sees her through the window, but does not dare to enter and departs. *Double Stars Shining in the Milky Way* was mildly successful, and it enabled famous director Sun Yu, who was merely a bit player in the film, to observe both Jin Yan, whom he had already discovered, and this young, vibrant, teenage singer and dancer Wang Renmei. It was then that he decided to make her a movie star.[6]

Notes

1. Wang Renmei, *Memoir: Wo de chengming yu buxing*, p. 21.
2. Short, *Mao: A Life*, pp. 164–192.
3. Wang Renmei, *Memoir: Wo de chengming yu buxing,* pp. 19–35.
4. Ibid., pp. 79–83.
5. *Encyclopedia of Chinese Films*, Volume 2 (1931–1949) (Beijing: China Movie Publishing House, 1996), p. 1222.
6. Richard J. Meyer, *Jin Yan: The Rudolph Valentino of Shanghai* (Hong Kong: Hong Kong University Press, 2009), p. 30.

CHAPTER 3

Overnight Stardom

Wang Renmei was excited that the filming of *Double Stars Shining in the Milky Way* had been completed. When she saw the finished film, she was horrified to discover that most of the sequences she had filmed were eliminated because of technical problems. Another disappointment for her was the dismissal by Lianhua of their singing and dancing group, which formally had been the Bright Moon Troupe. Fortunately for her, Li Jinhui reestablished the Bright Moon Troupe and Wang rejoined.

What could have been a happy occasion with the reformation of the troupe became a tragedy. The Japanese army, on September 18, 1931, planted a bomb, which blew up on the tracks of the Japanese railway in Manchuria. The explosion gave their military an excuse to occupy that part of China. Chiang Kai-shek told the Manchurian warlord, Zhang Xueliang, not to resist the invaders. The generalissimo wanted to save his army to fight the Communists who had set up a Soviet-style government in Jingxi the previous year. At the same time, Mao was elected chairman in 1931.[1]

The citizens of Shanghai were appalled by the events in the north. They all joined in an anti-Japanese boycott. Japanese goods were not purchased. By the end of 1931, their merchandise dropped to three percent of the city's total imported goods, from a high of almost one-third previously. Most Japanese-operated factories closed or stopped operations on a temporary basis. The Tokyo government was losing its patience with the unruly metropolis. Soon after, the Japanese placed Puyi, the Manchu, on the throne, as emperor of the puppet state of Manchukuo.[2]

Wang Renmei continued performing with the Bright Moon Troupe and joined their tour of the lower Yangtze Delta. At one of the performances, filmmaker Sun Yu saw Wang Renmei perform and remembered he had worked with her on *Double Stars Shining in the Milky Way*. He went backstage and asked her whether she would like to be in a film that he was writing. She, of course, was thrilled and wanted to know more. He told her that he was planning another film with Jin Yan and needed a co-star because Ruan Lingyu, who had been a famous co-star of Jin Yan, fled to Hong Kong when the Japanese, annoyed with the boycott, attacked Shanghai in early 1932. Sun and Jin were horrified by the imperialistic and aggressive attitude of the Japanese. They wanted to portray the Chinese in a film as strong in order to inspire the populace to fight the invaders. And yet, they hoped to do a film which would not be banned by Guomindang censors. Wang Renmei had an opportunity to become the new face of Lianhua and was thrilled to play opposite a heartthrob like Jin. Sun decided to cast Wang Renmei as Xiao Feng in *Ye Meigui* (*Wild Rose*). Once again, the poet of film demonstrated his talent in finding and developing inexperienced actors.[3] While waiting for shooting to begin, Wang continued to work on other projects.

The Bright Moon Troupe, after its tour of the Yangtze Delta, participated in two primitive sound films one of which entitled, *Bajiaoye Shang Shi* (*Poetry on Palm Leaves*) was shot by the Tian Yi Movie Company, but was a box office flop. The small film studio even tried to insert color during the musical performances orchestrated by Li Jinhui.[4]

Poetry on Palm Leaves, while a commercial failure, demonstrated the tensions between Chinese and American technicians. Tian Yi Movie Company had hired American sound technicians with American equipment but had to pay large amounts of money which they could ill afford. One of the American technicians always locked the recording equipment after its use. Situ Huimin, a Chinese assistant, asked if he could look at the equipment and was refused. Situ asked the main manager of Tian Yi to help him, but the manager also refused. One night, Situ and his cameraman opened the door to the recording room, trying to take a look at the machine. The American technician happened to pass by, saw the light from the window and entered the room with a handgun, forcing them to leave immediately. Situ, facing the handgun, said to him, "You were hired by the Chinese and the machine is in a Chinese studio. Why could your Chinese colleagues not take a look?" The Chinese cast frowned upon the American's arrogance and felt proud of Situ.[5]

Wang Renmei believed that the manager of the Tian Yi company, Shao Zuiweng, was responsible. He let the American engineers always get away with their mistakes, which forced the actors and directors to redo scenes again and again. He also accepted all of the requests of the Americans, no matter how expensive they were. Wang Renmei noticed that when she was shooting *Poetry on Palm Leaves,* Shao Zuiweng never respected the suggestions of the Chinese employees and only took the advice of foreigners. He also gave stupid orders to Situ and his commands often resulted in the recording having to be done over and over again.[6]

When Sun Yu and Jin Yan were discussing an upcoming film and the fact that Wang Renmei had been selected to play opposite Jin, they also discussed their anti-Japanese film, which Sun was writing at the time. Jin, very interested in the young Wang Renmei, went to see one of her performances as part of the Bright Moon Troupe, in which she sang and danced. Jin was horrified with what he had seen. He called Renmei and her cohorts, "those who flash their thighs in an erotic way for material interests." She was furious. However, she forgave him after she read an article that Jin wrote for *Movie Times*. In it, the film star mentioned the Japanese bombing of Shanghai and the Chinese loss. He appealed to the public by writing "that the artillery of imperialists are already aiming at our heads." He argued that "the development of Chinese movies cannot be separated from the actual issues of China and that the only way out is to unite all social forces to fight with the imperialism that is suppressing us." Wang Renmei was really impressed with his newspaper article and did not stay angry.[7]

Others, too, attacked the music written by Li Jinhui, director of the Bright Moon Troupe, and its use in many of China's first musical talkies. Young composer, Nie Er, felt that Li's music was not only materialistic, but appealed to the lowest common denominator. He shared his views with both Jin Yan and Wang Renmei.[8]

Cai Chusheng, a director for Lianhua, as well as an independent director, also met Wang Renmei on the set of *Double Stars Shining in the Milky Way*. He cast her in a film which he wrote and made very quickly in 1931 for the Heng Sheng Film Company. *Chunchao* (*Stirring of Love*, a.k.a. *The Spring Tide*) is about an old man in prison, reflecting on his early life. In his diary, he finds a rose which evokes sweet memories of his youth. In the story, Guo Hua is hired by a company in Nanjing to work as an engineer. As part of his assignment, he travels to Shanghai and on the way, takes the opportunity to visit his cousin, Yu Ying (played by Wang Renmei), who is going to school there. Yu and her younger brother, Shao Lu, are on their way home from a vacation. Guo takes them and their luggage along and accompaniess them home. During a welcoming banquet, the grace, charm, and laughter of his cousin, Yu, makes him think of a time of earlier pleasures. He misses his ride to Nanjing and learns that Yu has already promised herself to marry a man who has loaned money to the family. Guo decides to leave Shanghai immediately. Yu reproaches him for his love, but at the same time, her attitude shows that in fact her impending marriage is just for the sake of fulfilling the wishes of her mother. It has been forced upon her by her mother because of their poverty. Both Guo and Yu try to persuade Yu's mother to change her mind.

Yu's arguments with her mother are overheard by her fiancé Lin Yun. Lin scolds Yu and comes to collect the family's long acquired debt. Guo proposes that within two weeks he will pay off the family's debt. Guo bids farewell to Yu, promising to go to Tianjin to sell land in order to obtain the money necessary to pay back the debt. On the way, he randomly runs into his old classmate, Ma Xiang. When Ma hears about this matter, he persuades Guo to sell his land to Ma's rich wife.

Yu learns in a letter that the land will be sold and that Guo will return to Shanghai in two or three days. She is so happy that she jumps for joy. When Ma's wife meets the cultured and refined Guo, she tosses her husband by the wayside and tries to seduce Guo. He cannot resist the temptation and becomes the "plaything" of Ma's wife, Mei Li. Autumn comes and it has been months since Yu heard any news from Guo. Lin incessantly presses for repayment of the debt. Yu continually bites her lip and grinds her teeth to endure the humiliation. In order to get revenge on Guo, Ma tells the story of his corruption in Tianjin to the mother of Yu. Yu does not believe it. She longs for Guo's return. Her mother's dissatisfaction and the actions of Lin force Yu to go out on the long bitter road to Tianjin but when she is caught by Mei Li's servant in the middle of a field of snow, Guo is in the midst of his activities with Mei Li.

A few months of dissipation forces Guo's health to decline. Mei Li is also sick of him. She is looking for a new conquest. Finally, she kicks him out one day. After Yu returns home, the suffering and anxiety of her life have affected her health and she loses hope. Lin finally gets the police to come and seal up her home. When she hears that Guo has killed Mei Li, and that he is sentenced to life in prison, Yu commits suicide. The sweetness of his past memories and the pain of the present nearly drive Guo mad. In the final scenes of the film, he seems to see Yu smiling at him from the window. He tries to go forward to hug her, but the iron bars restrain his freedom. He falls and struggles with his remaining life. In the ongoing torrent of spring passions, Guo Hua and Yu Ying's entire lives have also passed away.[9]

Fortunately for Wang Renmei, this potboiler was not seen by many people. The film did make both writer and others more careful in choosing film studios to work with. Cai vowed to write a much better story for Renmei if she agreed to work with him again. They would have that opportunity when the pair teamed up again for Lianhua productions in two years' time.

Meanwhile, the young actress had the chance to make another film right away in her debut with writer and director Sun Yu. Sun welcomed Wang Renmei back to Lianhua. Jin Yan, her co-star, was anxious to play opposite this attractive and vibrant young girl in a film that would "get away" with their anti-Japanese message and promote Chinese nationalism. *Ye Meigui* (*Wild Rose*) was just the vehicle to elude the Guomindang censors.

The character of Xiao Feng, or "Little Wind," played by Wang Renmei, is the very essence of health, a wild girl full of vigor, who often unbinds her hair and bares her legs. (This kind of activity was criticized not only in the film but in the productions of the Bright Moon Troupe.)[10] Renmei in the role is headstrong and mischievous.

At the beginning of the film, she organizes the children of the district to imitate military exercises. The residents call her their "Wild Rose"—sweet, beautiful, and fragrant.

Her co-star, Jin Yan, plays a wealthy painter, Jiang Bo, who drives his expensive convertible to a small fishing village to sketch the countryside. He spots Xiao Feng having an altercation with a rich merchant who is trying to make advances. The girl pushes the lecher into the mud and gets dirt all over his face. The artist stops his car and laughs at the scene. She is not amused. He is captivated by her adorable, fresh, and unsophisticated behavior.

As the story progresses, she agrees to let him paint her portrait. When Xiao Feng's father has a fight with the merchant and knocks him unconscious, he leaves the hut, which later catches fire. The father is accused of murder and disappears. Xiao Feng is left homeless so Jiang brings her to Shanghai. Before taking her to his home, he stops to buy her city clothes and has her visit a beauty parlor. The scene in which she enters the mansion and keeps falling in her new high heels is hilarious. She fascinates the upper-class people in Jiang's home, but shocks them with her direct way of speaking. The guests feel humiliated. Unlike Pygmalion, Jiang cannot convert Xiao Feng from a country lass to a city girl. They are expelled from the house by the artist's father.

The pair, now in love, move into a slum dwelling with two friends. At first, they have a happy existence. When winter comes, Jiang becomes ill. They run out of money and face eviction. Xiao Feng finds the purse of a drunk on the snowy streets and returns home. When the police arrive, Jiang says he took the money and is also accused by the drunk. He is taken to jail. Xiao Feng goes to Jiang's father and promises to keep away from his son forever if he will help.

When the artist is released, she is gone. He returns to his upper-class life after searching for her unsuccessfully. China is being threatened from beyond the oceans (Japan is never mentioned because of Chiang's policy of appeasement). At a grand ball held in his mansion, the northeast military volunteer's song is heard from the parade on the street. Hearing the marshal music, Jiang yells at the people dancing, who have previously ignored the national crisis. He opens the window and spies his two old friends from the slums who urge him to join. The young man, attired in a tuxedo, leaps from the room onto the street where he joins the marchers. As he strides with the throng, he notices the back of a female volunteer with long hair. Jiang approaches and discovers it is Xiao Feng. Together, they march forward with an army of patriots.[11]

Sun's brilliant direction with magnificent country scenery and shot composition is highlighted by beautiful tracking shots that communicate the pace of events. The director used overhead shots and a crane to follow Jiang and Xiao Feng up and down the stairs to their flat. In addition to Jiang's driving a convertible, Sun showed him riding a motorcycle.[12]

When the film was released in 1932, Wang Renmei was referred to as "Wild Rose." The close working relationship between Jin and Wang soon led to them becoming lovers. Before audiences could see *Wild Rose,* the Japanese found another excuse for action. It was perpetrated when Japanese monks were "attacked" by a crowd in the Chinese district of Zhabei; one was killed and two wounded. The Japanese counsel general presented an ultimatum to the mayor: arrest those responsible, dissolve all anti-Japanese groups, and end the boycott in ten days or else their navy would occupy Shanghai. Chiang Kai-shek acquiesced but Japanese marines invaded anyway in late January 1932. The Guomindang army fought back but bombers from Japanese ships destroyed Zhabei. After five weeks, a truce was negotiated in May, which called for demilitarization.

The conflict, more popularly referred to as the "Shanghai incident," foreshadowed the events five years later, when the Japanese invaded Shanghai again and remained for eight years as an occupying force. Although the democracies of the world were outraged in 1932, little was done to come to China's aid. The United States protested, but President J. Edgar Hoover informed Japan that he would not resort to economic sanctions.[13]

When Shanghai calmed down at the end of May, several film studios were completely destroyed. In addition, 16 of the 39 cinema theaters in the city were in ruins. Most of the production companies were in deep financial trouble. Many of the directors and actors at Lianhua, including Jin Yan, were anxious to make an anti-Japanese film written by Tian Han, whose home had been destroyed by the bombing. Tian moved in with Jin. Later, Wang Renmei became a housemate as well. When introduced to Jin's "respectable older brother," she was a little nervous because of his reputation as a writer and anti-fascist. Tian brought her, Nie Er, the composer, and Jin to observe the actual fighting between Guomindang's 19th Route Army and the Japanese marines at the North Railway Station. They were impressed as the defenders fought back, even after heavy pounding by the invader's artillery. The battle continued for five weeks until the truce. All of them wanted to make a patriotic film right away, but Jin and others had other commitments.[14]

Although the premiere of *Wild Rose* was delayed by the bombing of Shanghai, when it finally opened, it was a success. The subtle message in the film where Xiao Feng taught the children to drill like military men using toy weapons and armor was not lost on the Shanghainese people. One of the inter-titles in the film has

Wang Renmei's character telling the children to "love China—the motherland." The movie was so popular that the press started calling her "Wild Rose" and clamored for her to make more films. With all the press adulation for her performance in *Wild Rose,* she yearned to star in another film. Her next activity was joining the entire staff of Lianhua Studios in the anti-Japanese film *Gongfu Guonan* (*Going to Aid the Nation Together*, a.k.a. *Coming to the Rescue of Our Country*). The plot is simple. It relives the events of the Japanese invasion of Manchuria and the subsequent bombing and aggression in Shanghai. Directors Cai Chusheng and Sun Yu and their crew presented a montage of Japanese soldiers advancing south of the Yangtze River to threaten Shanghai. In the film, after the Japanese soldiers have bombed the city, the aggressors are held off by the 19th Route Army. There is a conflict between those who support the Guomindang's position of appeasement and those who want to fight. One line from the film gives its message: "The war is unfortunately upon us. It is the very time that we ought to rise to the aid of our country." At the close of the film, a brother of one who is killed and that hesitated in fighting the Japanese joins the militia to save the country and heads to the front lines. Jin Yan's role is one of the militia and Wang Renmei is seen as a civilian caught up in the chaos. The rest of the cast included most members of the Lianhua Troupe.[15]

The film was written by Sun Yu and was directed by four of the major directors of the Lianhua Studios: Cai Chusheng, Sun Yu, Wang Cilong, and Shi Dongshan. In the patriotic fervor of the cast and crew, members of the company had many opportunities to interact on a personal level. Jin Yan and Wang Renmei had become lovers and were living together, and both Cai Chusheng and cinematographer Zhou Ke expressed a desire to work with her in a film in which she, now an overnight sensation, could star.

Her first opportunity came in late 1932 in a film directed by Cai Chusheng who had worked with Wang Renmei in *The Spring Tide*. Now, they were all back with Lianhua Studios making the film, *Duhui De Zaochen* (*The Morning of a Metropolis*). Wang Renmei plays Xu Lan'er, the younger sister of her brother Xu Qiling. The story is a typical melodrama which contains veiled criticism of the feudal society. On a cold early morning, the driver of a cart Xu Ada finds an illegitimate child abandoned by the road. He names the baby "Qiling." The infant grows up and gets along well with Lan'er, Ada's daughter, played by Wang Renmei. They love each other as brother and sister. Twenty-four years later, Qiling has become an architect and is employed by Huang Menghua Construction Company. One day, Huang Menghua, owner of the company, is inspecting the worksite and discovers that Qiling is actually the illegitimate child he abandoned at the time. What had happened is that three years after Huang Menghua had abandoned Qiling, he married a rich woman and had a son named Huiling. Huiling is an evil-tempered, vicious young man and his father despises the legitimate son because he does not try to improve himself. He wants to get to know Qiling in order for him to take over his business, but he is afraid of hurting his image of a gentleman and his standing in society. He does not dare to publicly recognize him, but only tries to help him out financially on a private level. Qiling is tough and determined; he refuses to accept a penny.

One day, Huiling also comes to inspect a worksite. By chance on that day, a young girl named Lan'er has also come to see her older brother. Huiling is startled by her beauty and starts to think of evil ways to harm her. He does everything he can to get her into trouble and finally comes up with a way to frame Qiling and get him put in jail, while Lan'er is taken away and put under house arrest. After a few days, the innocent Qiling is released. When he returns home, he finds that his father has passed away and his sister is confined to her bed. Burning with anger, he goes to the Huangs' house and begins a fight with Huiling.

Hearing the news, Huang Menghua, though sick, hurries home and says that he is sorry for his past mistakes. He begs Qiling to accept him as his father and he promises to give him one half of his wealth as inheritance. Qiling does not accept this and takes his badly injured sister to leave the scene of the crime. They walk off into the morning light.[16]

Although the film was screened in just a few theaters, Wang Renmei's portrait of the sister and her transformation from a bright, young girl to a sick, badly injured woman impressed the critics. *The Morning of a Metropolis* was well received. It was a sensation. Usually, in those years, films were put on during their first run for three to five days but *The Morning of a Metropolis* was screened for 18 days in succession. Wang Renmei had an opportunity to observe Cai Chusheng in his direction of *The Morning of a Metropolis*. This experience helped her in future films, since Cai was a stickler for detail. He always held a notepad and made sure that all of the actors were familiar with the script. He talked to each individual performer about the plot and requirements. For example, when she was filming a scene with her brother, he told her not to walk down the stairs but that she should slip down from a rope hanging from upstairs and she should play with her brother, conveying both naïveté and optimism. He also had great ideas during the shooting. For example, he made sure that Wang Renmei's character stood very close to her brother to indicate their warm family relationship.

At the height of *The Morning of a Metropolis'* popularity, Lianhua Studios received a letter from an ophthalmologist, stating that he had never seen anyone's eyes that looked like those portrayed in the close-up of one of the bit players who acted as a warm-hearted neighbor of Wang Renmei's character. Director Cai was not satisfied after several takes so he talked to the cameraman and decided to film half of the neighbor's face first and then the other half and combine the two takes. The result was that in the movie the neighbor opened his mouth with surprise and his two eyeballs turned in two different directions at the same time (one clockwise and the other counterclockwise). This so-called special effect made the audience extremely excited, according to Wang Renmei.[17]

With the great success of *The Morning of a Metropolis* and a positive audience and critical reaction, Lianhua Studios decided that it was time for them to make a full-fledged sound film and star in it its new discovery, Wang Renmei.

The film itself portrays Wang Renmei as her old characterization of "Wild Rose" as kid sister to Qiling. Also, the filmmakers used a wild rose in every scene with Wang Renmei, as well as with her brother's rich boss Huiling. The scene which later became a crowd pleaser shows an extreme close-up of the actress's eyes crying. Director Cai Chusheng made use of the close-up extensively in his later films.[18] Cai Chusheng and Wang Renmei worked so well together on *The Morning of a Metropolis* that the director told her he was planning another film which could take advantage of her singing qualities. This led to her most famous film, *Song of the Fishermen*.

Notes

1. Terrill, *A Biography: Mao*, p. 112.
2. Meyer, *Jin Yan*, pp. 29–30.
3. Li Suyuan and Hu Jubin, *Chinese Silent Film History* (Beijing: China Film Press, 1997), p. 346.
4. Andrew F. Jones, *Yellow Music* (Durham, NC: Duke University Press, 2001), p. 99.
5. Wang Renmei, *Memoir: Wo de chengming yu buxing*, p. 115.
6. Ibid., p. 117.
7. Meyer, *Jin Yan*, p. 39.

8. Jones, *Yellow Music*, p. 100.
9. *Encyclopedia of Chinese Films*, Volume 2, p. 1222.
10. Jones, *Yellow Music*, p. 101.
11. *Encyclopedia of Chinese Films*, Volume 2, p. 1190.
12. *Wild Rose*, DVD (San Francisco: San Francisco Silent Film Festival, 2009).
13. Barbara W. Tuchman, *Stillwell and the American Experience in China, 1911–1945* (New York: Macmillan, 1970), p. 137.
14. Meyer, *Jin Yan*, pp. 34–35.
15. *Encyclopedia of Chinese Films*, Volume 2, pp. 50–51.
16. Ibid., 2, p. 218.
17. Wang Renmei, *Memoir: Wo de chengming yu buxing*, p. 131.
18. *The Morning of a Metropolis*, 35 mm film (Beijing: Chinese Film Archive).

CHAPTER 4

Song of the Fishermen and the Creation of Wildcat

T he year of 1933 was to become known as "Chinese Film Year." Jin Yan was named "Emperor of Film" and Wang Renmei, because of her triumph in *Wild Rose* and *The Morning of a Metropolis*, was about to embark on a motion picture which would have international implications.

This new film for her that Cai Chusheng had developed was about extremely poor fishermen on the north coast of China. The director asked Nie Er to write a song that would embody the suffering of these exploited seagoing people. He knew that Wang Renmei could deliver the music in an empathetic way, thereby conveying the tormented lives of these working-class people.

After assembling the cast at the Lianhua Studios, thirty members of the group went to Shipu Village in Xiangshan County in eastern Zhejing Province. It was symbolic that they arrived by sea. Shipu was a declining fishing town with rundown houses. The crew and cast stayed at two inns that did not have electricity. The dwellings were ridden with huge insects which the citified actors found disconcerting. The original plan was to film there for one week, but actually the filming took more than one month. The production had many difficulties.

Cai could only find a small fishing boat for the shoot. Because of its size, it bumped and jolted on the sea. Many actors had motion sickness and the cameraman vomited so hard that he could not work. Wang Renmei, at the age of 19 and in excellent physical condition, did not feel very uncomfortable. In fact, she bonded with the fishermen and learned a great deal from them. She discovered how difficult their lives were.

The weather was another factor. It rained most days. Many of the cast and crew were sick. Many times, they could only stay in their fetid conditions and could not work.

The group was also bullied by the Guomindang cadres. Shortly after they arrived, the local gentry and the cadres held a reception for the group. However, the Guomindang and gentry merely wanted the group to entertain them by singing and dancing. The actors had to conform. After the reception, some of the "big shots" attempted to get close to the actresses in the company.[1]

Cai Chusheng and Nie Er stabilized the crew and actors by emphasizing the importance of the film. Whenever the rain stopped, filming would continue. Despite the pouring rain, some of the scenes had to be shot anyway. The inn in which the cast stayed had thatched roofs and leaked. The cast and crew bonded with the local fishermen and had long conversations with them. The fishermen told the cast how the local bullies lowered the price of fish and how poverty made them lose their children. Wang Renmei listened with tears in her eyes. Nie Er, when he wrote the music for the film, was inspired by the humble lives of the fishermen. The composer also had a part as a fisherman in the film, even though he had a high fever. When he became sick on the first take, everybody said that he did not have to redo the scene but he insisted on another take. His hardworking spirit moved the cast.

Wang Renmei played Xu Xiaomao, or "Little Cat." In preparing for the film, she learned to paddle a boat. She practiced many days until her arms were sore and swollen. She experienced the hardship of life in that tawdry village and heard sad stories from the local fishing people. She saw how the local gentry bullied the locals as well as the cast. What she saw, heard, and experienced helped her understand the mental world and inner feelings of Little Cat. When someone asked her the secret of her characterization of Little Cat, she said that she did not have any secrets. She said that because she experienced the life, thoughts, and character of Little Cat, she became that character. When she observed the life of the poor, she moved from mere compassion to a more complete understanding of their condition. She remembered that she played herself in *Wild Rose,* so it was not difficult, but in *Song of the Fishermen,* she improvised a new character.[2]

At the same time that Wang Renmei was undergoing hardships in Shipu, her lover Jin Yan was filming *Da Lu* (*The Big Road*), directed by Sun Yu. Both Jin's film and Cai's production were to have music by Nie Er and to have it heard for the first time, thanks to Diantong Equipment Company Limited, the first Chinese technical sound establishment.[3] Since the two productions were shot initially as silent films, the sound portion was later synched in the studios. The lyrics to *Song of the Fishermen* attempted to convey the suffering of the fishermen:

> Cast the net lightly, hold the rope tightly, wait for the traces of fish in mist and fog . . . fish are hard to catch but the rent and taxes are heavy: fish people remain poor generation by generation . . . dawn has come, and we are exhausted, yet our fishing village is still so far away. Waist is sore and hands are swollen, we caught fish but our stomachs will still be empty.[4]

When Wang Renmei sang the lyrics to the inhabitants of that small village, they were moved. Nie Er taught the inhabitants of Shipu the theme song from his other film, *The Big Road*, and worked with several of them to develop a troupe called "Big Road." Three members of that group went to Yan'an to follow the Communists and played a role in the propaganda campaign against the Japanese during the war.

Wang Renmei in *Yu Guang Qu* (*Song of the Fishermen*) played Little Cat, twin sister to a boy named Xu Xiaohou, or "Little Monkey." These were the nicknames of the children of Xu Fu, a fisherman who dies at sea after being forced to pay rent to the "Fishing King," He Renzhai. Mrs. Xu is forced to become a wet nurse to the "Fishing King" and suckle his son He Ziying, while caring for Little Cat and Little Monkey. Little Cat and Little Monkey grow up and carry on their father's work as fishermen. They do not own their own boats and must rent those of the He family when they do their fishing.

He Ziying follows in his father's footsteps and goes out and tries to learn about the fishing industry. He had grown up with the Xu children. When they go down to the seacoast, they all sing "Song of the Fishermen."

Soon after, the seaside village is attacked and pillaged by pirates, forcing the Xu children and their blind mother to wander until they end up in Shanghai. They live with an uncle and get by singing for money on the docks. He Renzhai also ends up in Shanghai. He starts a fishing company with foreigners and marries a social butterfly Xue Qiyun.

Two years later, He Ziying completes his studies in Shanghai and returns to the village where he is hired by the firm his father founded, Yanghua Enterprises. He discovers that the company's consultant, Liang Yuebo, is engaged in corruption on a large scale.

He decides to go to the fishing site to conduct further investigations. He unexpectedly encounters the Xu family on the docks. Because his ship is just leaving, he does not have a chance to talk to them so he pulls out a 100 yuan note and hands it to them.

On the way home, the Xu family passes by a bank that is being robbed. The police are in a shootout and their uncle is hit. Because Little Cat and Little Monkey are found to have a 100 yuan note in their possession, they are immediately suspected and arrested. That night, the uncle comes back from the hospital and he and his sister (the blind mother) are so distraught that they carelessly knock over a can of gasoline and are incinerated.

Meanwhile, He Ziying is able to find proof of the embezzlement of Liang Yuebo at the fishing site. He sends a telegram to his father. Mr. Liang finds that the game is up and notifies his accomplice, the social butterfly wife Xue Qiyun, and they flee with the family's finances. He Ziying returns to Shanghai and because he takes in the homeless Xu children, he and his father have an argument. As he is pressing his point one night, the whole shameless side of He Renzhai's terrible life is brought to light. Mr. He commits suicide out of shame.

Now that He Ziying's family has been destroyed, he realizes that he can never fulfill the hopes of changing the fishing industry, so he decides to become a laborer fishing with the Xu children. However, soon after, the overworked and weakened Little Monkey eventually collapses with exhaustion. The dying brother, at the very end, begs his sister to sing "Song of the Fishermen" one last time as the film closes.

Lianhua entered the film at the Moscow International Film Festival in 1935 and won an honorary prize. This was the first time in the history of Chinese film production that an international film festival awarded a prize to any Chinese film.[5]

The crew and cast returned to Shanghai to finish shooting some extra scenes and to edit the film. By this time, Wang Renmei discovered that she was pregnant and found it difficult to shoot some of the interior scenes since she developed swelling in her arms and legs. As production for both *Song of the Fishermen* and *The Big Road* neared completion, Jin Yan and Wang Renmei decided to marry. They wanted a simple and modest affair, not like those of other stars.

On the day of the wedding, Lianhua held a 1934 New Year's party. The couple came to the occasion wearing ordinary blue coats. When the bell for the coming year rang, they pulled red velvet cards from their pockets as Sun Yu announced that they were husband and wife. Wang Renmei recalled that their simple, modest wedding became a legend among young students of the time.

Unfortunately, Lianhua's chief did not agree. He believed that once a female movie star married, she would lose her audience. Wang's contract with the studio was not renewed but she was able to finish the filming of *Song of the Fishermen*. She also did not seek employment with other film companies until after her pregnancy was completed. Although she decided to rest at home instead of working, the active woman continued to play basketball and swim.

Jin was shooting *The Big Road* the night Wang Renmei had her baby. He rushed to her side the next morning and stayed with her all day. He was happy about the birth of the child, but was disappointed and sad when the infant died ten days later. Wang blamed a premature delivery for the demise of their son.[6]

Wang and Jin, although saddened about the loss of their child, were nevertheless delighted that their recent films, *The Big Road* and *Song of the Fishermen* were commercial successes. Both films opened to great acclaim in Shanghai and other cities where they were screened. After the premiere of *Song of the Fishermen,* audiences thronged the cinemas. The film played to sold out crowds for many weeks.

Wang Renmei received a new nickname from her performance in the film, which was "Wildcat." She remembered that when she was walking the streets of Shanghai, window shopping strangers would stop and look at her and it made her very uncomfortable. People would call out, "Here is 'Wildcat.'" She decided to dress in modest clothes and did not wear high heels or put on any makeup. She did not attend parties or go to bars. She wanted to keep a low profile and did not want to be "flashy."[7]

The commercial successes of their latest films gave Wang Renmei and Jin Yan new confidence. They decided to appear together in a play written by their friend Tian Han. *The Song for Returning Spring* had music composed by Nie Er. The story was about the Japanese bombing of Shanghai in 1932. Wang played the part of an overseas Chinese girl, Mei Niang, and Jin starred as Gao Weihan, a patriotic young teacher who was injured in the January 28 event and lost his memory. He regains his sanity later in the drama. Wang Renmei sang several songs written in the style that was prevalent in southeast Asia at the time. Earlier in her career, as a member of the Bright Moon Troupe, she had visited the area and realized that such songs were not difficult for her to vocalize.

During the run of the play in the fall and early winter of 1934, Tian Han sneaked into several performances undercover as he was hiding from the Guomindang police who were trying to arrest him. He told Wang how satisfied he was with both of their acting and singing presentations. Unluckily, Tian was captured shortly afterwards and sent to Nanjing. The couple did not learn about their friend's imprisonment until a few months later. A woman broke into the couple's living room, knelt down before them and started kowtowing and saying, "Please find a way to save Tian Han!" Wang Renmei was taken by surprise and she saw Jin Yan's face turn pale. When asked what was wrong, the woman stood up and said that she was Tian Han's lover.

Wang and Jin tried to use their influence to get Tian out of jail while they were still in Shanghai, but failed. However, the couple went along with a basketball team to Nanjing for a game and decided to use that opportunity to try to save Tian. Jin Yan went to see an official of the Guomindang and shortly afterwards Tian was released.

Tian Han, while free from jail, remained undercover. He completed a script, *Fengyun Ernu (Sons and Daughters of Wind and Cloud)*, and invited Wang Renmei to be the heroine of the film. It was made by the Diantong Film Company, which had a reputation as being a Communist organization. Many famous directors and actors did not dare to work for the company. *Sons and Daughters of Wind and Cloud* was the second movie the company made. The director was Xu Xingzhi and the music was written by Nie Er. The composer shared a great deal with Wang Renmei since he was a graduate of the Changsha Normal School and was born in the same city.

Wang Renmei plays the part of Ah Feng, a singsong girl. Her role was an example of how the left harnessed the pathos of this woman forced to sing bawdy songs for a living as a figure of oppression, national humiliation, and national resistance. Nie Er's song for the film, "The Singsong Girl Under the Iron Hoof," was sung by Wang. Ah Feng's song inserts a note of patriotic urgency into a scene that would have otherwise been indistinguishable from a host of other Chinese musicals of the era:

> Everywhere we sell our songs
> We perform our dances all around
> Who doesn't know that the nation's on the brink of disaster?
> So why have we been taken for courtesans?

> Because of hunger and coldness
> We sing our sad songs everywhere
> We've tasted all of life's cares
> Dancing girls are condemned always to drift
> Who's willing to be someone's slave?
> Who wants to let our homeland fall into enemy's hands?
> The singsong girl under the iron hoof is pitiful,
> Whipped until her whole body is torn and bleeding.[8]

Sons and Daughters of Wind and Cloud tells the story of a group of young people in Shanghai who, driven by social disorder and external threat, either sink into lives of dissipation or resolve to devote themselves to the anti-Japanese war effort in the north of China. The film climaxes with a stirring rendition of the song that was to become Communist China's national anthem. Nie Er's "March of the Volunteers" was set to a sequence in which a group of peasants pledge themselves to militant resistance.

Ah Feng, an orphan child compelled by poverty into a career as a singsong girl, eventually redeems herself in the struggle against military encroachment. The film follows Ah Feng on a tour with her song and dance troupe to the seaport of Qingdao. After the troupe regales theater-goers with a Spanish inspired dance routine, Ah Feng's song "The Singsong Girl Under the Iron Hoof" inserts a note of patriotic urgency into the scene. Implicit in the film is the notion of redemption—the implication that the oppressed singsong girl is ready and willing to be enlisted to the cause of national salvation. In the final scene, by the side of the Great Wall, Ah Feng and her friends, along with crowds of soldiers and civilians rush towards the enemy, singing the "March of the Volunteers."[9] (Unfortunately, the sound quality is poor.)

Wang Renmei and her friend are reunited at the Great Wall in this final scene. Director Xu Xingzhi used a Soviet-style montage, showing calendar pages flipping across the screen to indicate the passage of time, and that Wang and the poet had met before in an earlier scene when he was a student. In addition, Xu used a montage of people fleeing a war scene. Many of the leftist films of the day were influenced by Soviet social realism as demonstrated by these techniques.[10]

Although Wang Renmei did not have her contract with Lianhua Studios renewed, director Wu Yonggang asked her to appear in a very small part in the film *Xiao Tianshi* (*Little Angel*). The movie directed by Wu has Wang Renmei as the sister of the leading man, Ge Zuozhi. The reason Wu was able to bring back Renmei was that his first film for Lianhua, *The Goddess*, was a box office sensation and has been considered one of the top ten Chinese films ever made. Because of his success, he had influence at the studio.

The script for *Little Angel* was based on an Italian writer's work written for children entitled *Education of Love,* which was published in 1866. It was translated into Chinese in the 1920s. Wu wanted people to read that book because he believed people should love children and promote the beauty and the spirit of young people. He thought their spirit could change the whole society with their force. Consequently, he made the movie to promote the book. Although Wang Renmei did not have a lot of scenes, she was impressed with the young actor Ge Zuozhi, who starred in the film.[11]

The actress, by this time famous, was asked to star in a play titled, *Huichun Zhi Qu* (*The Song for Returning Spring*). Throughout her career, she had the ability to move from screen to stage because of her extensive experience with the Bright Moon Troupe as well as the success of *Song of the Fishermen.*

Her husband, Jin Yan, was also at the height of his career as a male star in Shanghai with the screening of *The Big Road,* which was finally censored by the Guomindang. The Lianhua Studios, loyal to the Guomindang, made another film supporting Chiang Kai-shek's New Life Movement. However, the company failed to raise enough capital because of worldwide depression and ceased most productions.[12]

Both Jin and Wang were ready for new challenges. Flamboyant impresario and producer Zhang Shankun recruited them along with several directors from Lianhua Studios, including Bu Wancang and Wu Yonggang, as well as Shi Dongshan. Zhang called his newly formed film company Xinhua Productions (New China Movie Enterprises). He received funding from gangsters of the Shanghai underworld. Zhang also had the reputation of being a rogue businessman and was a member of the notorious Shanghai mafia organization known as the "Green Gang." Sometimes he invested in good movies. However, he did not hesitate to produce "quick and dirty" pictures with, as one critic recalls, "unhealthy content."[13]

The new head of Xinhua was known as quite a publicity hound. His take-off of *Phantom of the Opera*, the successful Hollywood movie starring Lon Chaney, was a big hit. He placed a phony story in a local tabloid paper that a child died of fright after seeing the film. In the scene from the movie where actors are on the stage, they delivered revolutionary messages which somehow avoided Guomindang censorship.

Wang Renmei was excited that her first film for the new production company, *Changhen Ge* (*The Song of Perpetual Regret*) was to give her a starring role, in which she sang several songs. The picture itself was designed to be a vehicle to show off the very popular singing style of Wang, who had issued several recordings of her songs which were purchased all over China.

Reunited with director Shi Dongshan, Wang Renmei plays Ma Nina, the daughter of a wealthy tea merchant who kicks her out of his mansion for refusing to marry the son of another rich merchant.

She travels to Shanghai with Zhu Dongxin, her lover, so he can work for his uncle, a rubber dealer. When Zhu comes home drunk and is suspected of cheating on Ma, she abandons him and becomes a singer in a radio station. The director of the radio station, Hong Nanping, gets involved with Ma and finally moves in with her. Meanwhile, Zhu, hearing his old flame on the radio, proceeds to the station and has an altercation with the station director. A few days later, Zhu goes to Ma's home and berates her whereupon Hong pulls out a gun to threaten her former lover. The two wrestle for the gun, it goes off and Hong is killed. Zhu is arrested and sentenced to death. Ma is also captured and put into jail. At the film's climax, she hears with great grief the firing squad's gunfire, signaling the death of Zhu Dongxin, and she collapses on the floor of her cell.[14]

Wang Renmei and her husband Jin Yan were reunited in a film directed by the now famous director Wu Yonggang, *Zhuangzhi Lingyun* (*Soaring Aspirations*). Wu cast Jin as Shun'er, a village leader and Wang as Black Clown, his lover. Together, they lead the villagers to rise up and fight back many times against countless attacks by bandits. In a series of fights, they win constantly, but because the ammunition runs out, they have no choice but to sacrifice themselves as heroes. Shun'er is overwhelmed with sadness and in the midst of battle as Black Clown is killed, he takes an oath to attack to his last breath. Holding in his hand a weapon, he leads the villagers on to fight as the film ends. His last words are, "If we retreat, where would we go? This is our land."[15]

In one scene of the film, the flag of the Republic of China (Guomindang) is raised over the village. Wu deliberately used the flag to goad Chiang Kai-shek to stand up to the Japanese instead of fighting the Communists. Mao Zedong, by this time, had reached Yan'an after the Long March. The Communist leader advocated a united front against their common enemy. That would have to wait until the outbreak of World War II.

The success of *Soaring Aspirations* encouraged the director Wu Yonggang. He immediately wrote another script entitled *Huanghai Dadao* (*Pirates of the Yellow Sea*). The director had a chance to anticipate what was to happen several months later in 1937. The plot about pirates referred to the Japanese. The story was about passengers encountering pirates at sea and their resistance. That summer, while the cast including Wang Renmei, was shooting the film in Qingdao, news reached them that Japanese troops skirmished with Chinese soldiers at the Marco Polo Bridge just outside of Beijing. On July 7, 1937, the invaders used the excuse that one of their soldiers was kidnapped by the Chinese. Later, the serviceman was found in a brothel and returned by the Chinese to his commander, but it was too late. Thousands of Japanese troops poured into northern China. The Marco Polo Bridge incident gave the invaders an excuse to begin an undeclared war against China.

The film company hurriedly returned to Shanghai to finish the film, only to discover that by August 12, the Japanese had sent 26 warships up the Huangpu River with its flagship, the cruiser *Izumo*, moored directly in front of the foreign settlements. Thousands of Japanese marines had landed and ousted the settlement police, declaring authority over all of Hongkou, which was then part of the International Settlement. All Japanese civilians were evacuated to Japan. Next, they systematically bombed population centers in large Chinese cities.

Hundreds of thousands started to flee Shanghai. Many Chinese attempted to reach the International Settlement thinking that the invaders would not bomb the Westerners' territory. Meanwhile, British and American citizens were preparing to board evacuation ships. Other refugees tried to leave on steamers headed upstream. Chinese airplanes tried to sink the huge Japanese vessel *Izumo*, missed the target and dropped bombs on crowded sections of the city, killing and wounding thousands of Chinese and foreigners alike.

The fighting ensued for over two months with the Chinese forces completely overpowered. Tokyo sent an additional 200,000 troops. The battle raged for Shanghai and millions of refugees were forced to sleep on the sidewalks, while the lucky ones made it to the International Settlement, which was not involved in the battle. Between 1937 and 1939, about 750,000 Chinese fled to this "haven of tranquility." Even after the capture of Shanghai, the Japanese did not take over the settlements.[16]

The Japanese entered Nanjing on December 12 and discovered that Chiang Kai-shek and the Guomindang had left, leaving the city undefended. During the next six weeks, Japanese soldiers raped and murdered about 300,000 civilians with relentless violence. The "Rape of Nanjing" is still remembered in China and is a sore point between the two countries.

Shanghai, however, was spared the same fate because the Japanese only controlled the Chinese portion of the city. The international settlements remained in European and American hands. The foreign enclaves were surrounded on all sides by the Japanese and were named the "lonely island" and "orphan island." By the end of the year, it was business as usual in the settlements, whose neutrality was respected by the Japanese. However, Japanese soldiers guarded the entrances to the settlements and required all Chinese that entered to bow down to them or else they were beaten and even killed.[17]

The Shanghai film studios were shut down during the battle, but as soon as calm was restored, Zhang Shankun reopened his Xinhua facilities and filming was completed on *Pirates of the Yellow*

Sea. Censorship now was even greater since the Japanese consulate requested that the Guomindang government prevent the shooting of certain movies and the Chinese government obeyed. *Pirates of the Yellow Sea* starred Wang Renmei, and although the film is mostly talk because of the problems with filming on location in Qingdao, the film's music again demonstrates not only Wang's singing but includes a fishermen's chorus which portrays the extremely difficult life of a fisherman.

The story is one that tends to be convoluted, but Wang Renmei is radiant as she looks at the moon on the deck of an ocean liner with a large group of tourists and with the knowledge that there is $500,000 in cash in the vessel's safe. All is peaceful until sounds of gunshots are heard, which leads to chaos among the passengers. A pirate ship comes close. The ocean liner's crew, the passengers, and the pirates are locked in combat. In the end, the pirates get control of the ship. They use their weapons to force the captain to point the ship in the direction of a lonely island. The leader of the pirates orders the captain to give him the cash but is refused. Instead, he turns on the guests and forces them to hand over their watches and cash. One of the passengers, who is actually a pirate disguised as a civilian, has already taken the $500,000 and tells the pirate chief.

When the vessel reaches the lonely island, fishermen are hired to transport the pirates and their prisoners to the secret island. The fishermen complain about foreigners who speak another language, who fish with mechanical means and prevent the local fishermen from plying their trade with traditional methods, and as a result, many of them are forced to become pirates. Wang, in her role as the beautiful Miss Lin Qing, tries to reason with some of the pirates and tells them that that is not the way to live. The pirates force the hostages to write to their families for ransom.

Lin Qing and another passenger decide to persuade the prisoners to escape from the island but she sends a friend to contact the authorities for help. He is immediately pursued and both boats run aground. The hero takes the gun away from his pursuer and kills him. The police hurry down and arrest the pirate chief. Not long after, the police rescue the kidnapped passengers on the island. The passenger who shot the pirate is sent to prison and Lin Qing will wait for him when he returns.[18]

Unfortunately for the cast, *Pirates of the Yellow Sea* was screened but received little attention from the public and the press.[19] Most of the attention was focused on the new occupiers of Shanghai—the despised Japanese.

Notes

1. Wang Renmei, *Memoir: Wo de chengming yu buxing*, p. 137.
2. Ibid., pp. 138–141.
3. Jay Leyda, *Dianying, Electric Shadows: An Account of Films and the Film Audience in China* (Cambridge, MA: The MIT Press, 1972), p. 95.
4. Wang Renmei, *Memoir: Wo de chengming yu buxing*, p. 145.
5. *Encyclopedia of Chinese Films*, Volume 2, p. 1255.
6. Meyer, *Jin Yan,* p. 49.
7. Wang Renmei, *Memoir: Wo de chengming yu buxing*, p. 54.
8. Jones, *Yellow Music*, p. 126.
9. *Encyclopedia of Chinese Films*, Volume 2, p. 257.
10. *Sons and Daughters of Wind and Cloud*, 35 mm film (Beijing: Chinese Film Archive).
11. Wang Renmei, *Memoir: Wo de chengming yu buxing*, pp. 180–182.
12. Li and Hu, *Chinese Silent Film History*, p. 393.
13. Wang Renmei, *Memoir: Wo de chengming yu buxing*, pp. 221–222.
14. *Encyclopedia of Chinese Films*, Volume 2, p. 77.
15. Ibid., pp. 189–190.
16. Poshek Fu, "Between Nationalism and Colonialism: Mainland Emigrés, Marginal Culture, and Hong Kong Cinema 1937–1941," in Poshek Fu and David Desser (eds.), *The Cinema of Hong Kong:*

History, Arts, Identity (Cambridge: Cambridge University Press, 2000), p. 201.

17. Meyer, *Jin Yan*, p. 67.
18. *Pirates of the Yellow Sea,* 35 mm film (Beijing: Chinese Film Archive).
19. Wang Renmei, *Memoir: Wo de chengming yu buxing*, pp. 188–189.

CHAPTER 5

Exodus from Shanghai

All of the Shanghai movie actors were upset with the Japanese invasion. They decided to put on a play and work jointly to present *Defending the Lugou Bridge*. Both Wang Renmei and Jin Yan played parts in the production which was about the incident at the Marco Polo Bridge on July 7. Thousands of Shanghainese swamped the Penglai Theater which was close to Xiao Ximen in the Nanshi District in Shanghai. Each performance was sold out with all the tickets going in just ten minutes. Wang Renmei was so busy with the performances that she did not even have time to have dinner, but because of the patriotic nature of the play she said she was not hungry. The actors and the audience shared one thought—they did not want to be the slaves of Japanese invaders in a destroyed country. The show lasted from August 7 until August 13. After that, many of the actors left Shanghai and joined a troupe visiting different parts of the free territory of China and entertaining troops. That left a gap in the lives of Jin and Wang.

At the same time, most of the major movie companies stopped doing business. In the first half of 1938, only Xinhua was still making movies. The boss of the production company Zhang Shankun was only concerned with making profits. Because the political situation had changed, he resorted to horror and erotic movies. Under those circumstances, it was impossible for both Jin and Wang to make any serious movies with progressive themes. Zhang, noted for his fast production methods, had Jin make three films in that year. The "Emperor of Film" was unsatisfied with all of them. Wang Renmei starred in the film which was designed for her singing talents, *Li Hen Tian* (*Parting from Heaven with Sorrow*). Director Wu Yonggang asked Wang Renmei to play two roles: a mother named "Rose" who eventually dies, and her daughter "Little Rose." The supporting cast was mainly actors from the former Lianhua Studios who had remained in Shanghai.

The opening shots of the film depict various scenes from a circus with rolling credits superimposed. The circus troupe in the film goes to its various locations by ship. The opening scene shows Wang singing on the deck of the ship with a song about the soft moonlight and laments that her youth will not return. She explains her plight to a friendly sailor and is beaten by the boss of the circus, played by Zhang Zhizhi, the professional villain of early Shanghai movies. Suddenly, Rose is protected by two of her clown friends. In another scene, the sailors from the ship visit the circus in Shanghai after having become acquainted with the crew. The director used wipes between the various acts of the circus. It is apparent that in order to make a quick film without spending a lot of money, the boss of the studio actually filmed a real circus.

Wang Renmei sings about roses again as part of the circus act. She also dances in the final scene. Finally, Rose leaves the circus and moves in with one of the sailor's sisters. However, the sailor, who has been supporting his sister, is jailed, so Rose is forced to return to the circus. She faints during a performance while singing because she is pregnant. With ill treatment, she dies and the two clown friends raise her daughter Little Rose.

In a scene reminiscent of old Hollywood B movies, the circus boss falls after tripping on a rug, stabs himself, and dies. The two clowns take over and run the circus. Little Rose sings in the circus and looks just like her mother. Obviously, the role is played by Wang Renmei. The final scene is at the grave of Mother Rose. At the end of the film, Rose sings as the camera scans the skies. We do not see Rose but her spirit at the grave sings the melody.[1]

Writing in her memoirs, Wang Renmei was apologetic for the film but reflected that the film did show people from the lower social classes, although the plot was a cliché. It was not well received by the audience and the actress felt that she was responsible because of her limited acting capacities.[2]

Wang Renmei's husband, Jin Yan, was also unhappy with his various roles. He started drinking whenever he was off the set. In one of his drunken moods, while walking with Wang, he noticed a billboard promoting actress Gu Lanjun whose name appeared above that of Jin's for his film *Wu Song and Pan Jinlian*. He pulled down the ad, ripped it up, and smashed the billboard. His wife told people that his behavior was understandable because it was caused by "an explosion of all of the pains and hardships Jin Yan had suffered as an actor longing for social progress." Wang always came to the defense of Jin Yan when he was drunk.[3]

Even in wartime conditions, Jin and Wang's popularity continued. The Japanese approached Jin Yan as "the only male superstar . . . remaining in Shanghai." The couple realized that the occupying forces wanted to use him for propaganda purposes and made plans to escape to Hong Kong and then to Chongqing, where they were assured there would be more films for them to make.

During this time, an underground war between Guomindang agents and the Japanese puppet regime occurred between 1937 and 1941. Both sides murdered one another as well as journalists, businessmen, and politicians who were suspected of either cooperating with or resisting the Japanese. Kidnapping, theft, and crimes of all kinds surged. Newspaper offices were bombed or set on fire. The boss of Xinhua decided to register his company in the United States in order to evade Japanese harassment. The Shanghai press had done the same thing in registering their publications abroad as "foreign published." It became extremely hazardous for Jin and Wang to remain in Shanghai, even though Jin was relatively safe because of his reputation and popularity.

Their plan to leave Shanghai for Hong Kong was made secretly. Since they were both well-known actors and popular celebrities, they could not just buy tickets on the night boat to the British colony. They could not obtain proper documents from the Japanese because it would arouse suspicion. Instead, the couple went on board the steamer to say farewell to some friends at a going-away party, which was a custom at the time. In the cabin, Wang and Jin switched clothes and papers with their accomplices, who were friends from the insurance business. When the purser shouted "all ashore that's going ashore," the other couple in Wang's and Jin's costumes descended the gangplank and disappeared into the crowd.

Many exiled film people traveled to Hong Kong. The British colony housed many of the actors between 1937 and 1945. Several used Hong Kong as a stopping place on their way to Chongqing, Guilin, and other parts of China. Some pro-Guomindang filmmakers traveled back and forth between Hong Kong and Guomindang-held areas during the war.

Sun Yu, the director who had discovered both Jin Yan and Wang Renmei, was in Chongqing developing a story about the Chinese air force. His aim was to show its bravery against the superior numbers of the Japanese squadrons. The director knew that Jin was planning to arrive soon and planned to offer him a leading role. The Guomindang government needed the film medium to lift the morale of its citizens since the Japanese had, by 1940, conquered all of the eastern part of China and continued to push westward. The film industry as it existed was now working for the same goals as the Chinese government.[4]

While in Hong Kong, Wang and Jin associated with the film crowd who still remained there, many of whom decided to go to Yan'an to join the Communists, who were fighting the Japanese. The couple had that offer from Sun Yu and decided that they would go to the war time capital of Nationalist China.

Both of them later expressed regret that they did not go to join forces with Mao and therefore both had lost the chance to join the revolution at that time. The real reason why they did not go to Yan'an was that they really could not abandon their comfortable lifestyles as movie stars. Evidently, that life was too easy or it numbed their willingness to travel for the cause in less than ideal conditions.

Writing in her memoirs, Wang Renmei said that her lifestyle was determined by their new social status because they both came from a poor background. As they became richer, their lives got farther and farther from those of the impoverished people. She recalled her husband, Jin Yan, went from an extravagant lifestyle to one of self-indulgence and got stuck there more and more. "This type of life softened our wings, eroded our souls, and made us unable to abandon everything we already had and join the actors to go to Yan'an."[5]

In 1939, Wang and Jin flew from Hong Kong to Kunming to shoot the film *Changkong Wanli* (*Ten Thousand Mile Sky*, a.k.a. *Wings of China*), which was the first film made about the Chinese air force. Kunming was selected because Chongqing was continually bombed by the Japanese and all of the studios and editing rooms there were underground. Some productions were shot outdoors during the winter months, as the city was protected by thick layers of fog and enemy air raids usually ceased.[6]

Wings of China features Jin as Jin Wanli, a young athletic coach at Qilu University in Jinan who enlists in the Chinese air force. After the Japanese has bombed Shanghai, Jin and his fellow pilots vow to revenge the motherland. In a dogfight over the Yangtze River, they shoot down enemy planes. One of his buddies is injured in the attack and goes to the hospital. Later, the Japanese return and Jin straps himself into his airplane to pursue them. The Japanese retreat, but not before they bomb the hospital. The aviator's friend is killed. His little sister, played by Wang, also dies. As the enemy approaches again, the brave pilots take to the skies to avenge their fallen comrade.[7] Editing of the film took about two years because production was hindered by a huge bureaucracy, poorly educated censors, and meager financial help from the government. There was little incentive for filmmakers.[8]

The couple returned to Hong Kong at the end of 1940 and settled down in Kowloon. Jin began studying architecture, which he had done earlier in life, and Wang Renmei worked on her typing skills in English in order to assist her husband with his correspondence courses. At the same time, she participated in the preparation of a film and actually shot some scenes for the movie *Chun Hui Dadi* (*Spring Returning to the Earth*). The film was never finished because the Japanese invaded Hong Kong in late 1941.

Wang and Jin never expected that Hong Kong would fall into the hands of the Japanese army since the British were defending their colony, but the battle raged for several days. The couple, together with Wu Yonggang, went into hiding in the storage room of a Chinese bank in central Hong Kong. For two days and two nights, they did not have any food or water. They were so hungry that Jin and Wu risked their safety to go out and find food. Unfortunately, they were caught by Japanese soldiers when they came out of the bank. They were forced by the occupying soldiers to perform slave labor such as carrying water and cooking. Luckily, the two escaped, came back for Wang, and sneaked out of Hong Kong.

For over two months, they walked from Hong Kong to Guilin through Yulin and Liuzhou covering over 500 Chinese *li*, i.e. about 150 miles. Suddenly, they felt as one with the masses. They traveled with other refugees and suffered hunger and coldness with them. That experience got them closer to the ordinary people. In the past, they thought they were just progressive artists beyond criticism. Now experiencing personally, as refugees, the hardship and misfortunes of life brought by the Japanese invasion, they realized how comfortable their previous lives had been and how distant they were from the lives of the ordinary people.

Wang Renmei felt guilty and painful and regretted not joining the actors who went to Yan'an but they vowed to do something for the resistance movement. Jin decided to go to Chongqing to find an acting job. Wang remained in Guilin to wait for the news from Jin Yan. He had tried to report to the Central Movie Making Company in the wartime capital hoping to participate in films against the Japanese but the central propaganda department of the Guomindang did not welcome the actor.

Wang Renmei could not find a job in Guilin as well. However, she stayed with a friend of Jin Yan's and his wife, and took care of their four children who called her "Auntie Wang." Cai Chusheng and Situ Huimin, friends from the Lianhua days, were all in Guilin so Wang visited them often. They too did not have jobs. Wang Renmei remained in Guilin for eight months and at the end of 1942 went to Chongqing to be reunited with Jin Yan. Because they did not have their own house, they stayed with Wang's big brother, Wang Renxuan, and she took care of the household chores for the family. After a year, Jin joined a troupe entertaining the soldiers. In the spring of 1944, Wang Renmei returned to Kunming to join the Da Peng Troupe and starred in the play *Kongque Dan* (*Peacock's Gallbladder*). She also starred in another production, *Tianguo Chunqiu* (*The Spring and Autumn of the Heavenly Kingdom*).

The acting group in which Wang Renmei starred disbanded. She felt that one of the reasons was her acting skills. She believed that her performances in both plays were mediocre. Playing a Mongolian princess was something she did not understand. In addition, she was worried and anxious to develop characterizations in her roles, but she could not. "I felt that passion was not enough for an actor; one needs rich knowledge, and cultivation in art and great skills of acting to be a great actor."[9]

Fortunately, while staying with a close friend and hoping to find a job, Wang Renmei was told that the supply department of the U.S. army base in Kunming needed an English typist. Since she had English typing experience when she helped Jin Yan study architecture, she applied for the job and got it. Since the United States was an ally, she believed she was also contributing to the anti-Japanese war effort. Her hardship as a refugee influenced her decision not to worry about being a star. She decided that she could live the life of an ordinary person working with her hands, which she applied to the typing job.

In March 1945, she moved to the dormitory of the supply department of the army base and lived a collective life with many people. She worked basically as a secretary. She and her husband, Jin Yan, had been separated off and on for many months during the period of the last few years of World War II. Not being together may have been the reason that she received a letter one day from Jin, who was still in Chongqing. The curt note asked Wang Renmei for a divorce. He had been irritated that his wife had joined the drama company in Kunming and had also worked for the Americans. They had also had an ongoing problem with his drinking and her being stubborn, "there was no tear dropping and quarreling in our divorce."[10]

Wang was really not surprised when she received the letter asking for the divorce which she had been thinking about for a long time. She agreed. The alienation between the couple had been growing rapidly. They did not have a child and no longer had an emotional communication. However, although they divorced, they remained friendly for the rest of their lives. They never said any nasty words against each other after their break-up.

In November 1945, the U.S. military supply office where Wang worked moved to Nanjing. The actress said goodbye to Kunming with tears and flew back to Shanghai. During the eight years of warfare she lost her title as a movie star and a warm family, but she did receive recognition of her own ability and self-confidence. She believed that if she could return to the movie industry, work hard and study the art of acting, she could renew her former career. And she knew she could always use her hands to make a living. "Her hardships hardened her wings."[11]

She became a courageous "wildcat" flying towards a new life after the victory of the Chinese against the Japanese.

As her plane circled Shanghai, she looked at the city from above and felt that she was given a new opportunity to start life again. She remembered her youth when her siblings became revolutionaries but she became a singer and dancer. She recalled the friends who went to Yan'an to follow the CCP but she missed her chance. Now, leaving Kunming, she was full of confidence as the plane descended towards that international city. The plane had a bumpy landing, which Wang Renmei thought symbolized her life's path up until that point.

When she found lodging in Shanghai, she got a job as an English typist for the government. She worked there for three months before director Fei Mu visited her and asked her to star in a movie called *Jinxiu Jiangshan* (*Beautiful Rivers and Mountains*). Fei had been a director at Lianhua and was quite famous. During the war, he stayed in Shanghai making films with some of the Austrian exiles who resided there and then he escaped to Hong Kong. In Shanghai again, he told Wang Renmei that the film they were about to make was quite positive. It was about the construction of China after the war. She was thrilled to be working with such a great director. In her spare time, she practiced horseback riding, which was to come in handy later in her career when she was shooting the film *The Dawn of River Meng*. They went to Suzhou to shoot exterior shots and several outdoor scenes but after shooting for only a few days, Fei Mu ceased production. Wang was perplexed. Finally, Fei stopped the production completely.

Wang went back to Shanghai to continue her study of English. She waited for Fei to return and continue the shooting. She went to his home and asked whether it had been her acting that was the reason the director had stopped filming. "No," he told her. The reason was simple. He wanted to make a film persuading the various parties, Communists and Nationalists, into cooperating to rebuild the country but the country was now on the verge of a civil war. There was no sign for peace. How could he continue the movie? Wang was disappointed but she understood Fei's motives, since he was a very patriotic director. He had refused to work with the Japanese and Guomindang traitors.

At the end of World War II, the Americans had flown Chiang Kai-shek's troops into Shanghai and other enemy-held territories so that Mao's forces could not gain access to the major metropolitan areas. The Japanese cooperated with the Guomindang and kept their soldiers on the streets of Shanghai until American and Guomindang forces arrived.[12]

Under the Guomindang after the war, Shanghai was completely demoralized. Economic production had decreased sharply, inflation was out of control, the army was ineffective, and the government was corrupt.[13] A civil war between Mao Zedong's forces and the Guomindang appeared eminent. North China and Manchuria were in the hands of the Communists, while the major cities were controlled by the Guomindang thanks to the American assistance. However, many filmmakers and actors who had been away from Shanghai, like Wang Renmei, decided to return there hoping to become part of the motion picture industry once more.

The Guomindang government had appropriated more than 200 companies from broadcasting stations to shipping companies with no compensation given to the original owners. Government monopolies ran almost every area of enterprise in Shanghai. Chiang Kai-shek's personnel seized the excellent motion picture equipment that the Japanese had left behind and took over all of the film studios. Some of the actors and directors who had remained in the city during the occupation fled to Hong Kong, which benefited greatly from the talent and capital for the city's postwar construction.[14]

The Guomindang censors were stricter now than they had been before the war and most left-wing movie people left for Hong Kong when it was obvious that they could not produce progressive films. Those who remained and had infiltrated the hostile environment of Chiang Kai-shek's studios were called "heroes without battlefields" and "May Fourth Petty Bourgeois Inteligentsia" by Mao.[15]

Wang Renmei was losing confidence in the future of the country. At that moment, a director from the Kunlun Company invited her to star in a movie, *Guanbuzhu De Chunguang* (*The Spring That Cannot Be Confined*, a.k.a *Boundless Spring*). She was thrilled with the opportunity to star again and resume her career. If any film could reintroduce Wang Renmei to the Chinese audience, *Boundless Spring* was it. She had the lead as a female performer, Mei Chunli. The plot takes place during the War of Resistance and Mei is the lead performer of the China Musical Troupe, which carries out propaganda work entertaining troops on the front line. During a retreat, Mei is separated from the group and meets a speculator businessman, Wu Jingzhi. In the midst of the chaos, the two of them decide to travel together. Wu courts Mei and by the time they reach Chongqing, they are husband and wife. After a while, Mei receives a letter from the traveling troupe, hoping that she would come back to work with them at the earliest date possible. She is excited and replies to the letter saying that she is willing. Her husband, on the surface, supports her but secretly takes the letter of reply from the musical troupe and tears it into pieces. Later, he cuts Mei off from all outside communication.

When one views *Boundless Spring,* it plays like a Hollywood *film noir* movie. The opening is a long tracking shot with shadows, as a man carries a body up a long flight of stairs and then throws a woman in a room and locks the door. He tells a neighbor that his wife is insane and dangerous. She awakes and sees them drive off. Then, she sits down in a darkened room and remembers happier days in a flashback that sets up the story. Wang's voice is still lilting. She sings the title song, "Boundless Spring," over scenes of the natural views of the country. She also plays and sings for her husband. It is interesting that in that year, before Hollywood did, a double bed was used for the husband and wife.

It is obvious that Wang had matured as a serious actress, and was no longer limited to childlike roles. The banquet scene in Shanghai, where she refuses to sing, is one filled with great complexity. The phrase, "get rid of pests," appears over and over again which might refer to the civil war, which at that time was raging.

The director, Wang Weiyi, used superior production values in the film. He took a lot of time to reintroduce Wang Renmei. The actress' athleticism in the escape scene, climbing out of the window in the rain, is extremely realistic. The progressive nature of the film is evident when the gangsters from the city are "just like the pests." It is obvious that these references were aimed at the Guomindang.[16]

After the War of Resistance is won, Wu and Mei return to Shanghai. Wu takes advantage of the misery of the country, reflecting conditions that actually occur in Shanghai. His business becomes even more successful. Four years later, on the anniversary of his marriage with Mei, he holds a big banquet. After getting drunk, she is asked to get up on the stage and sing. She refuses, turns her back on the banquet, and leaves.

The conflict between Wu and Mei begins and escalates severely as the film goes on. In order to placate her after an argument, he satisfies her request and goes with her to an experimental farm to look around. Some of the farmers are those who were originally performers with the China Musical Troupe. Mei meets up with her old friends and the atmosphere is exuberant. Later, Mei is locked up in the villa by her husband after a fit of jealousy.

On a rainy night, Mei is able to rip the window curtain into strips, tie them together, and escape through the window and go back to the experimental farm. In a wonderful, musical setting, the farm holds a grand arts festival. Mei sings the song, "Boundless Spring," and garners great appreciation from all. Wu has brought with him a band of cutthroats and plans to seize and carry off Mei, but the farmers rise up to fight them off and protect her. Wu and his cronies are crushed. At the end of the film, Mei again returns to the farm and starts a new life.[17]

The outdoor scenes of *Boundless Spring* were shot in Hangzhou. For Wang Renmei, it was memorable. She joined a party show at

Zhejiang University with the college students. She sang for them "Song of the Fishermen" and "Solidarity in Strength," but in the middle of the performance the power went out. She believed that it might have been sabotaged by the Guomindang but no one panicked. Instead, the audience and singers together finished the songs in the darkness. She was ecstatic. She felt she had gone back to the days when she was shooting *Wild Rose*. She was in her thirties, extremely active, like a wildcat, and in the movie scene when she escaped from the villa, she had to jump from a very high window onto the ground in high heels. She whipped away the shoes during the course of jumping and landed on the ground with bare feet. It seemed that the old Wang Renmei had returned.[18]

The movie was shown in Shanghai in November 1948. The audience was pleased, and so was Wang. She believed, watching the film as a member of the audience and hearing their applause, that her performance was now on a different level. Playing the character Mei Chunli, she regained the self-confidence that she had almost lost and began believing again in the future of China and its people.

The left-wing nature of this film, however, made the Guomindang increase its persecution of progressive elements in film generally and in other performing industries as well. Many cultural workers left to go to the Communist-controlled areas or to Hong Kong on a temporary basis. Wang returned to Hong Kong and her former boss, Zhang Shankun, was there. He was now running the Hong Kong Great Wall Movie Company. He asked her to join a remaking of a 1927 film, *Wangshi Sixia* (*Four Knight-Errants Surnamed Wang*). Wang Renmei agreed because she had seen it when it came out and felt the story was beautiful and romantic, and also because she needed the money. However, after she joined the team she discovered the movie was quite different from the original one. Zhang was an opportunist. He just found four actors and actresses surnamed "Wang" and thought that was it. Other actors and actresses included Wang Yuanlong, Wang Yin, and Wang Danfeng.

Wang Danfeng was a young actress. She was famous because she had starred in a 1941 remake of *Song of the Fishermen*. However, that film was poorly made; the costumes were funny and looked like Mongolian clothing, and the movie was not attractive to the audience at all. The same was true of the film *Four Knight-Errants Surnamed Wang*. Wang Renmei was embarrassed because the 1949 version of the film was so different from the one made in 1927, but the Shanghainese audience remembered the original and therefore went to the movie. However, when they watched the film, they booed and she regretted having made such a film.[19]

At that time, Wang Renmei joined a reading group which was composed of artists and other cultural workers in Hong Kong and those who came from the mainland. They read the works of Mao Zedong, and discussed the readings and current politics. On October 1, 1949, a dinner was given by the group celebrating the official birth of the People's Republic of China. Because the Hong Kong government prohibited the meeting and assembling of large groups, any organization which was composed of over five people had to register. However, the reading group met using different guises, such as a birthday party or a wedding anniversary.

In December of that year, Wang Renmei heard that when the Guomindang fled Shanghai for Taiwan after the Communists took over, very few film personalities went with them because they had little sympathy with the Guomindang rule. Some of them had little knowledge of the Communist Party, or they had worked with their representatives but they had faulted the Chiang Kai-shek government for letting too many American films into China and permitting the Shanghai industry to suffer. They embraced the Communist Party's anti-American position and believed that they would be more assertive. The Communists actively recruited film professionals to their cause. After the occupation, movie and stage personalities welcomed liberation with a colorful parade.[20]

The entrance of the People's Liberation Army into Shanghai impressed the inhabitants. The soldiers had orders not to bother the population. The troops were mostly young teenagers, who had never been to a city and they slept on the sidewalks. The Communist Party took over the police force, who pledged cooperation.[21]

One of the first things the Communist Party did in Shanghai was to take over the two major Guomindang film studios, but the message went out that private film studios were still needed. The new Communist film studio, Shanghai Film Studio, needed time to gear up. The majority of performing artists as well as all of the major film stars participated in a massive parade to honor the People's Liberation Army.[22]

That year, Shanghai had 48 movie theaters. Twenty-two were first-run venues and all were privately owned and operated. Even though the Communists had taken over, hundreds of pre-revolutionary films were still screened between 1949–1951. The film veterans of Shanghai were thrilled with the initial moves by Mao's government and actively supported the movement against "poisonous" Hollywood films.[23]

Wang Renmei could not wait to return to the mainland, since she was devoted to Mao Zedong and his revolution. Before leaving Hong Kong, she joined a group from the Hong Kong movie circle which was invited to Guangzhou to view the new order. There were dozens of members in the group. They prepared drums and rehearsed dancing, singing, and plays ready to entertain the People's Liberation Army. Wang sang and danced with everyone when she saw a street full of red flags and heard drum music. She thought back to the street scenes she had observed during the great revolutionary period in Wuhan in 1927.

The mayor of Guangzhou and the PLA commander-in-chief welcomed them with a banquet. The city leader greeted Wang, holding her hand, and asked her to sing "Song of the Fishermen," and tears flowed from her eyes with excitement. While she was in Guangzhou, she was visited by a man named Chen who tried to persuade her to go to Taiwan where Chiang Kai-shek and millions of Nationalists escaped after the civil war. He told her that living standards there were high and the motion picture industry there would welcome her. "I told him I wanted to stay in the mainland." Then, another man named Zhang wanted to talk to her and she realized he too was an agent of the Guomindang. The spy said that her Hong Kong movie colleagues all supported the Communists, which was why the Guomindang needed her. He praised the worst movie she had ever made, which was *Four Knight-Errants Surnamed Wang*. She told him, "If you want to make anti-Communist movies, I won't cooperate with you."[24]

In the summer of 1949, the first Chinese National Literature and Art Workers' Delegation Conference was held in Beijing. Mao welcomed them and said, "You are all what the people need . . . we welcome you." Even though Wang Renmei was in Hong Kong, she was elected as one of the representatives in the delegation, so she returned to Shanghai in early 1950. She was greeted with 50 books as gifts from members of the Chinese National Literature and Art Workers' Delegation. Wang was grateful and determined to work hard to repay the Communist Party and the Chinese people for their overtures.[25]

Noting that there were no opportunities for her to make films in Shanghai, Wang went to Beijing to visit Tian Fang, the head of the Beijing Film Studio and also the vice-dean of the Central Movie Bureau. He was extremely warm with Wang. Tian told her that there were so many movie actors gathering in Beijing and suggested that she go to the Changjiang Movie Company in Shanghai. Wang landed a part in the film *Liangjia Chun* (*The Double Spring*, a.k.a. *A Spring for Two Families*).

It is ironic that Wang Renmei's part in the film was to be subservient to the role of Jin Yan's new wife, Qin Yi. Qin, as the lead, played Zhui'er, a lovestruck young woman who marries and falls in love with someone else. She tries to get out of her unreasonable marriage but cannot do so, and becomes very ill. The head of the women's ward, played by Wang Renmei, tries to help Zhui'er through talking and educating her. With that help, the sick woman finally musters her courage and decides to get a divorce from the man she does not love. The elders of both families communicate at length and gladly consent to a divorce. In the midst of laughter and joy, Zhui'er and the man whom she loves take their seats on a carriage and gallop off into the boundless farmland. The film was a good example of how the Communists were open to divorce and yet were attempting to show that families should communicate before they took such a step. The movie won third place in the Cultural Ministry's awards for that year.[26]

Qin Yi and Wang Renmei became very friendly during the filming of *The Double Spring*. In fact, Qin liked working with Wang because she was such an extrovert. Qin actually believed that the actress lived up to her nickname "Wildcat." She recalled that before liberation, she made several films and she was really outgoing and exuberant, and that was the reason why Jin Yan liked her. In addition, she had a vibrant and enthusiastic personality.

Qin recounted that Wang Renmei, with her small role, had plenty of free time. While the others were shooting, Wang would go to the countryside and buy local goods that farmers were selling (such as liquor or chicken livers). She would then bring them back and give them to Qin saying, "Jin Yan likes these; take them back to him."

According to Qin Yi, Wang Renmei still regretted her divorce from Jin Yan. She believed that the separation was caused by her bad temper, and when they fought, "she would just go off." During the later parts of the filming, Qin Yi noticed that Wang became depressed. Jin Yan's new wife said that it was unfortunate that Wang Renmei could not get over her nostalgia for Jin Yan, yet the two maintained a very open and warm friendship.[27]

When Wang returned to Shanghai after the filming, she received a medal for her appearance in the movie but lamented that her character suffered from a lack of depth, even though she appreciated the encouragement from the party.

Wang Renmei decided to become part of the struggle with the working people of this new Communist society, so she joined the Land Reform Work Team. On the night of November 30, 1951, she traveled from Shanghai by train to Bengbu on the bank of the Huai river in Anhui Province. They were greeted by a crowd and she sang for the welcoming party. They then left Bengbu to Huaiyuan County and dwelled in the cultural hall of the county, which had once been a temple. She and the group studied there for 19 days, and then went in smaller teams to the countryside to organize land reform. Wang's team went to Xinshang Village in Shagou District. The leader of the team was Han Jingchang from Shanghai, and Zou Bingqian, a local cadre. Wang was appointed the woman commissioner. The group convened all the local cadres in order to meet with them. In the next seven days, she talked to the local women, trying to understand their situation and mobilize them to fight with the landlords. Many poor peasants were surnamed Wang, so they felt intimate with her. She became friendly with many of the local wives, shedding tears for their hardship. She was extremely happy when they were emancipated.

This experience of land reform educated Wang Renmei, and with her experience at Shipu Village with Cai Chusheng previously, she believed that decline and disaster were in the past. Now with the land reform experience and her time with the Land Reform Work Team, she saw hope for the future.

While she was working with the local peasants, she fell ill and developed a fever. Despite her sickness, she managed to join the Bitter Telling and Struggle Meetings, which organized peasants to mobilize to fight the landlords. So she joined in the work of class clarification and redistribution of the property of the landlords. Though she was sick, she was happy. In February of 1952, she returned to Shanghai because her illness was not getting any better and she learned that she had pulmonary tuberculosis. Although she received shots for three months and recovered, she believed that her nervous system was hurt by that experience.[28]

After Wang had felt better, she participated voluntarily in the Zhengfeng movement which was organized in the cultural industry. This so-called movement was actually a purge of intellectuals. Although she was still feeling remnants of her illness, she was enthusiastic about going to the meetings on her own initiative.

Three months later, Wang became psychotic and started to talk nonsense. She was sent to the Minxing Mental Illness Hospital. She believed that the diagnosis was a side effect of the medicine she was taking and of her experience with the Zhengfeng movement.

Wang Renmei was not alone during this purge of intellectuals. Directors such as Sun Yu and many of the 1930s Shanghai movie circle were blamed for many of the ills of society. Later that year,

Wang Renmei's second sister took her to Beijing to receive treatment, and she lived with her older brother and was looked after.

As soon as Wang Renmei recovered from her mental illness, she wanted to work again. In March of 1953, she attended the First National Movie Art Work Conference, which was held by the Film Bureau in Beijing. After the meeting, she requested that she be given work in Beijing and was able to join the Beijing Film Studio. In September, she joined the newly established Beijing Movie Actor Troupe. She rehearsed many plays and started to study the art of acting systematically by studying the process and theory of character rendition.

The Changchun Film Studio invited her to join the making of a film, *Menghe De Liming* (*The Dawn of River Meng*), where she was given the role of the military doctor, Su Hong, which was not a large part. The film itself was about the period immediately following liberation and told the story of the Guomindang soldiers who were trying to incite a major conflict between two tribes near the river Meng. However, the PLA intervenes and prevents further bloodshed when they have a surprise attack on the enemy forces, killing all of them in one stroke. The movie was obviously an anti-Taiwan propaganda work since it shows the enemy parachuting down to attack the Communists before they are defeated.

The film was shot in the Tibetan area of northwestern Sichuan. When they were filming, they had to live in a small inn made of wooden logs. The entire area was still primitive. The cast showed a film to local Tibetans and when Mao appeared on the screen, all of the Tibetans applauded. When the chairman's image faded out, the audience did not have any idea what was going on, and went to the back of the screen to look for him. The movie team could not complete the showing of the film.

Wang Renmei was moved by their respect for Chairman Mao, but she was pained to see the backwardness of these people. She could not imagine that there could be a place this poor and backward after the liberation. She believed this was a corner forgotten by civilization and felt more pressed to do more to change the situation.

From that time on, Wang Renmei started to take notes analyzing the psychology of characters, designing the gestures and facial expressions of the various people with whom she came in contact. In the past, she had followed her intuition to act, but now she applied the class theory that she had learned in her participation in the land reform into the theoretical analysis of her characters, combined with the acting theory she had learned in the troupe. She now believed that she had a more profound understanding of characters she would play in future films. On the other hand, she sometimes made the mistake of using this concept to replace life itself. For example, when she performed as the military doctor, Su Hong, riding on a horse on a mountainous road, she believed that since Su Hong was a member of the PLA, she had to be heroic. So every time she was on horseback, she kept her body straight at ninety degrees towards the ground. That is naïve because members of the PLA are human too. They feel tired, and they show they are tired. In any case, Wang Renmei learned a lot from her part and moved on from acting as intuition to understanding it as an art.[29]

After finishing *The Dawn of River Meng*, Wang Renmei realized that the eight private film studios still functioning in Shanghai were shut down and their staff members were integrated into the expanding area of the state sector of filmmaking. Many of the film professionals who tried to adhere to the new regime were viewed with suspicion. The era of private sector filmmakers and privately owned theaters ended. The reason that the Communist Party had permitted these private film studios and actors to perform was that they needed more experience in the area of mass media. This ended with the showing of *The Dawn of River Meng*.[30] In addition, after three years of being run as a Communist city, Shanghai, the former sin city of Asia, was transformed. Mayor Chen Yi was quoted in *Renmin Ribao:*

> In the past three years owing to the persistent efforts of the people, Shanghai has changed from a city dependent upon the imperialistic economy for its existence to a city independent of the imperialistic economy and which is developing on its own. Shanghai is no longer a city serving the imperialists and reactionary elements but a city for the people and production. Shanghai has wiped out the dirt and poison left behind by the imperialists and their running dogs and has started on its way to normal and healthy development.[31]

At this time, Wang Renmei became acquainted with Ye Qianyu, a famous painter. Meeting at a social engagement, she remembered that he had drawn a caricature of her in a newspaper during the 1930s when she was known as "The Wildcat Actress." He portrayed her in the drawing as a dark skinned girl dancing the hula. When she had seen it in the 1930s, she laughed out loud and now meeting him in 1953, they soon developed a warm relationship. She watched him as he went to the park and various tea houses, where he drew sketches of people around him. He became so focused that he forgot that she was with him.

They decided to get married in 1955 when he was 47 and she was 41. The news of the wedding spread all over Shanghai. Friends came and congratulated them with gifts. She could not refuse them but the couple wanted to repay the various people who had given them gifts. Ye said, "Let's have a party in a restaurant," so they went to a fancy Sichuan restaurant with dozens of their friends. Ye spent over 200 RMB. On the way back, he told Wang Renmei that he had just become bankrupt because all he had was the 200 yuan. She had to laugh, but from then on she had to buy all of the groceries with her own money because the artist never saved any money.[32]

According to Qin Yi, Wang Renmei was the artist's second wife. He was famous as a newspaper cartoon and comic artist, but he had been married to a ballerina who later ran off with another ballet star and left him alone. At that point, he decided to court Wang Renmei and finally he won her. However, after their marriage, he always remembered, missed, and thought about his former wife.

He did not treat Wang Renmei very well. Whenever something came up, Wang Renmei, being very impulsive, would walk into Ye's studio and try to tell him everything. He did not pay any attention to her. It finally got to a point when he did not even want to talk to her.[33]

Wang Renmei admired Ye very much. After the marriage, he read every night, often into the midnight hours. As he was also the chair of the National Painting Department of the Central Art College, he was kept busy with administrative issues in the daytime and could only read at night. She was very understanding. Ye studied important traditional paintings repeatedly and he also studied the painting theories of other countries, such as those in Europe, Japan, India, and Persia. He had a broad interest. He was interested in music, dancing, and photography, and his paintings later in life were sold for large sums.

Wang Renmei remembered that Ye was a good painter but not a good husband. Ever since they were married, she took care of everything in the house (shopping, cooking, and cleaning). She put up with him because of her background and accepted him as a creative painter who had only one thing in mind—to paint. She suffered in silence—it was not easy to be the wife of Ye.[34]

During the time of her early years in marriage, she was still a member of the Beijing Film Studio. Although she did not get parts in films, she was assigned various tasks such as National Election Mobilization work in Fusuijing in the Xicheng District of Beijing. She was part of a three-member team: one was a guard from the Zhongnanhai; another was the head of the police station in Fusuijing. One day while the group was walking, she met a Buddhist nun in the street who called her name. Wang Renmei recognized that the nun had been an actress in one of her past movies, *Sons and Daughters of Wind and Cloud,* over twenty years ago. Wang was so happy to see her and chatted with the woman. She discovered that the nun had had such a horrible life that she became a devout Buddhist.

The leader of the team looked at them with suspicious eyes. Immediately after the nun left, he yelled at Wang, asking how she could know a Buddhist nun: "What was your relationship with her?" The actress was stunned by those questions. But the head of the police said, "Wang Renmei was an actress from the old society, so she has a complicated social network and knows many people, but she herself may not be that complicated."[35]

The incident with the nun is a good example of how the Communists from Yan'an treated the actors and actresses who were stars from the old Shanghai. They were considered "yellow," which meant "salacious and obscene." The Bright Moon Troupe, for example, was considered a pornographic organization and therefore she and some of the others could only get small parts in films because they were considered untrustworthy and part of an evil social network.

In 1956, the Communist Party held a meeting to further indoctrinate so-called intellectuals. In the summer of that year, Wang Renmei went to Qingdao to study Marxism and Leninism. She was then recruited to go to Guangdong and Suzhou to recruit more film actors to learn about Marxism.

At the end of that year, she was rewarded with a part in a stage play, *Family*. Although she was 42, she was assigned the part of a 17-year-old girl. Wang was worried about her ability to play this part well but she grabbed at the opportunity in order to prove herself. She studied the character of the young girl really hard. She delved into the relationship between experience and rendition. The play's director helped her. She had always played film characters more closely aligned with her real-life personality, but with this new role, she entered into the character of Ruijue, who was a good wife and a mother marked by self-sacrifice. The character was presented as a young woman eager for a happy life.

The play *Family* was well received in Tianjin. Both in the city and the countryside, the audience did not want her to leave after the play had finished. They remembered the film *Song of the Fishermen* and always requested her to sing the theme song from that film. She told the audience, "I made some movies about working people but those were not satisfying. I hope I could play a character that truly belongs to the working people."[36]

With the success of her performance in the play, she was given an opportunity to play in the film *Qingchun De Jiaobu (The Steps of Youth)*. The film was shot at the Changchun Film Studio in the spring of 1957. Wang played Shufang, the wife of an engineer. She is a humiliated spouse, later abandoned by her husband. However, the story is a good example of a sophisticated production which showed "the new China."

In the opening sequence, there are new buildings everywhere. The basic concept of the motion picture is that the old bourgeois ideas of design, in terms of building and architecture, are pitted against a practical Maoist style of economic planning. When we first see Wang Renmei, it is apparent that she has gained weight. In the plot, Wang Renmei's husband, who is an architect, fools around with one of his students. It is apparent that he is a philanderer. At a student dance, they sing about spring. The sequence had excellent production values.

The student, impregnated by Shufang's husband, takes medicine to have an abortion. The girl feels regretful, ashamed, and takes a huge amount of the medicine, which could have been fatal, but fortunately is discovered soon after and saved. With the assistance of the criticism of the leaders and comrades, the student recognizes her mistakes and resolves to start a new life. The evil husband, with his reprehensible behavior, is subject to law and punishment. The student recovers, and with many comrades, returns to the work of architecture and throws out the bourgeois style of the errant husband. She is encouraged to lift her spirits, change her errors, and work for the future.[37]

The film demonstrates the propaganda at the time pitting the petty bourgeoisie against group think. Group criticism of the individual was necessary. "A strong sense of individualism has hurt you and you should seriously change your life" was the view of the group to the student after her abortion. The actions of the husband and his involvement with the student were portrayed as wrong because of their petty bourgeois thoughts, not romanticism. The film was considered a great propaganda success. English subtitles were included in the film as it was circulated to Europe and other English-speaking countries.[38] It was thrilling for Wang Renmei to be part of this feature film and to have once again a major role. She looked forward to more opportunities in the future.

Notes

1. *Parting from Heaven with Sorrow*, 35 mm film (Beijing: Chinese Film Archive); *Encyclopedia of Chinese Films*, Volume 2, pp. 527–528.
2. Wang Renmei, *Memoir: Wo de chengming yu buxing*, pp. 192–193.
3. Ibid., pp. 193–195.
4. Meyer, *Jin Yan*, pp. 68–72.
5. Wang Renmei, *Memoir: Wo de chengming yu buxing*, pp. 207–208.
6. *The New York Times*, June 14, 1942.
7. *Encyclopedia of Chinese Films*, Volume 2, pp. 299–300.
8. Poshek Fu, *Between Shanghai and Hong Kong* (Stanford: Stanford University Press, 2003), pp. 38–40.
9. Wang Renmei, *Memoir: Wo de chengming yu buxing*, pp. 219–220.
10. Ibid., pp. 222–223.
11. Ibid.
12. Stella Dong, *Shanghai: The Rise and Fall of a Decadent City* (New York: Harper Collins, 2000), p. 280.
13. Lloyd E. Eastman et al., *The Nationalist Era in China, 1927–1949* (Cambridge: Cambridge University Press, 1991), p. 176.
14. Fu, *Between Shanghai and Hong Kong*, pp. 135–140.
15. Paul Clark, *Chinese Cinema: Culture and Politics* (Cambridge: Cambridge University Press), pp. 5–19.
16. *Boundless Spring*, 35 mm film (Beijing: Chinese Film Archive).
17. *Encyclopedia of Chinese Films*, Volume 2, p. 308.
18. Wang Renmei, *Memoir: Wo de chengming yu buxing*, pp. 231–232.
19. Ibid., pp. 232–233.
20. Paul G. Pickowicz, "Acting Like Revolutionaries: Shi Hui, the Wenhua Studio, and Private-Sector Filmmaking, 1949–1952," in Jeremy Browne and Paul G. Pickowicz, eds., *Dilemmas of Victory: The Early Years of the People's Republic of China* (Cambridge: Harvard University Press, 2007), pp. 256–288.
21. Fredrick Wakeman, Jr., "Clean-up the New Order in Shanghai," in Jeremy Browne and Paul G. Pickowicz, eds., *Dilemmas of Victory*, pp. 21–59.
22. Pickowicz, "Acting Like Revolutionaries," p. 262.
23. Ibid., pp. 262–263.
24. Wang Renmei, *Memoir: Wo de chengming yu buxing*, p. 235.
25. Ibid., p. 236.

26. *Encyclopedia of Chinese Films*, Volume 2, p. 574.
27. Interview, Qin Yi, July 4, 2009.
28. Wang Renmei, *Memoir: Wo de chengming yu buxing*, pp. 251–253.
29. Ibid., pp. 254–255.
30. Pickowicz, "Acting Like Revolutionaries," pp. 260–263.
31. Mayor Chen Yi, Shanghai, May 28, 1952, quoted in *Renmin Ribao* (People's Daily), May 31, 1952.
32. Wang Renmei, *Memoir: Wo de chengming yu buxing*, pp. 242–243.
33. Interview, Qin Yi, July 4, 2009.
34. Wang Renmei, *Memoir: Wo de chengming yu buxing*, pp. 237–250.
35. Ibid., pp. 255–256.
36. Ibid., pp. 257–258.
37. *Encyclopedia of Chinese Films*, Volume 2, p. 764.
38. *The Steps of Youth*, 35 mm film (Beijing: Chinese Film Archive).

CHAPTER 6

Chaos in China

Returning to Beijing, Wang Renmei was delighted to become a part of the Beijing Film Studio and joined the Chinese Movie Association. At a celebration, the members of the group went to the Forbidden City to meet with members of the government. Mao Zedong entered, took one look at Wang Renmei, motioned for her to come over, and asked her if she still remembered her home in Changsha. Wang had not expected that the chairman would remember her after all those years. He recalled the wonderful experience he had when living with her father and all of her brothers, sisters, and family members. She thanked Mao for his support of the film industry and thanked him for sending a hard-cover copy of his works to her brother's wife when she could not find the copy anywhere, because it was sold out.

She had learned about the book earlier because when Mao visited Shanghai, he asked someone to look for her at the Shanghai Film Studio and instead met Wang's sister-in-law. This meeting with Mao was prescient because during the great famine later, she and her sisters and brothers were invited to dine with Mao at Zhongnanhai.

Indeed, during the Cultural Revolution, both Wang Renmei and her niece were assisted by Mao.[1]

All of the members of Wang's film company were delighted when the Hundred Flowers Thaw started. During this period, all intellectuals and party members were asked to examine the party in order to improve it. However, when the Hundred Flowers Thaw ended, those who spoke out were attacked as "rightists."[2]

Wang Renmei was able to start filming *Tanqin Ji* (*The Story of Visiting Family,* a.k.a *Story of Visiting Relatives*) in which she did not have many scenes, but in flashbacks she played a young village girl. Wang was concerned about her age and presumably her weight as well, but the director encouraged her by saying that in front of the camera she did not look old. With some makeup, she presented herself as a maiden. The actress was happy, feeling like she did during her youthful years.

The Story of Visiting Family is fairly simple. It tells the tale of a long journey to Beijing by a father looking for his third son, with whom he has been separated for over ten years. His son has gone to a remote province for work. The father later discovers that the person when he thinks is his son is actually not. What has happened is that another boy and his son are close comrades in the army. During the battle, the father's brave boy has been killed but his friend continues to write his father from the battlefield using his name and treating the old man as if he were his own father. When the old man realizes he has lost his own son he is extremely saddened, but he is moved by the high ethics and bravery of his son's friend. In this way he is comforted.[3]

While the group was shooting *The Story of Visiting Family,* the anti-rightist movement reached its height. The studio was forced to change the theme of the movie, as it should not be critical of how Communist Party cadres betrayed their countryside bias after they came to the city to become officials. The story was changed to praise the People's Liberation Army veterans who helped support old people. All around Wang Renmei, fellow actors and directors were being accused of being rightists. She was shocked that her loyal Communist Party friends were pointed out as enemies because they had probably said something wrong in the meetings and had made some critical remarks during the Hundred Flowers Thaw.

Wang made the mistake of supporting one of the actors who, she said, had been an early supporter of the revolution in the 1930s. She was implicated in the criticism. She recalled that her attacks were "like a flat ball lacking air." Her mental problems came back again. She became hysterical and was hospitalized in 1958. She believed that there was always deep prejudice against people with her background. Her experience with the Bright Moon Troupe and the Shanghai film industry in the 1930s made the young cadres distrustful of her and she was looked down upon.

When Wang Renmei returned from her hospital stay, she learned that Mao had established the Great Leap Forward. Since the People's Republic of China's first five-year plan (1953–57) was successful, with the GNP increasing 9 percent on average each year, Chairman Mao set a goal of doubling output. All sectors of the economy were to be involved. The film industry was included in the movement, along with agriculture, steel, and coal—all major enterprises and even backyard furnaces. The government established even more film studios, this time in smaller cities. Film production for the entire nation increased from 82 features in 1956–57 to 187 films in 1958–59. Many movies were shot quickly and were of poor quality. It is estimated that more were produced than actually noted. False reporting of fantastic results was given to the government by factories and agriculture communes. The newspapers, controlled by the government, announced achievements every day and the public was exhorted to produce more and more. For example, in 1958 steel production was 8 million tons, short of the 11-million-ton goal, since 3 million tons of the steel were unusable, having been made in the so-called backyard furnaces. It was the same problem in agriculture. Wang did not mind the Great Leap Forward because it meant more opportunities for her and her colleagues to make movies. However, before her next film assignment, she appeared in the play *Fuchen* (*Surfacing and Sinking*) with the Beijing Movie Actors Troupe.

Wang Renmei, by this time playing middle-aged roles, is the mother of the lead character Lin Daojing's best friend in the film *Qingchun Zhi Ge* (*The Song of Youth*). The plot begins in the early 1930s when Lin, a student, refuses her arranged marriage and flees to relatives who will not give her help, so she throws herself into the sea to commit suicide. She is saved by a Peking University student, becomes his colleague, and later marries him. She leaves her husband and comes under the influence of the Communist Party student member leader, and with his help starts to read revolutionary books and take part in revolutionary activities. Her husband, from whom she is now separated, is unhappy and jealous. She decides to leave her husband for good, joins the revolution, and is kidnapped. A Communist secret agent helps her to dress up as a man so that she can escape. Later in the film, she teaches in a primary school in a village and becomes close with the leader of another youth movement. Under his leadership, she establishes a revolutionary movement among the peasants and this alerts the enemy to her work. After she returns to Beijing, she takes part in the student youth movement but is betrayed by a traitor and sent to prison. While she is incarcerated, she receives an education from a female Communist Party member, Lin Hong, played by Qin Yi, who is later executed. After Lin Daojing gets out of prison, she joins the Communist Party and leads the student movement against the Guomindang.

It is ironic that Wang Renmei, although having an extremely small role, plays in the same film as Jin Yan's current wife, Qin Yi.[4] The production values of *The Song of Youth* were better than many other films of that era. A symphonic score accompanies the opening shots of the sea with themes of the "Internationale." Additional music is provided by songs sung by the refugees as they are forced to flee by the Japanese. A chorus is heard in the background as Lin Hong is led to her death.[5]

When Wang Renmei returned to Beijing after shooting *The Song of Youth,* she learned that her uncle's son had died and that she had missed the funeral. Her cousin was a well-known revolutionary who had accompanied Mao to Beijing and went overseas with many of the young members of the Communist Party in the 1920s. Zhou Enlai, for example, studied in France while her cousin went to the Soviet Union and became a citizen. He had returned from the Soviet Union with his Russian wife and children several years before, and Wang and Ye visited them. Ye made a charcoal drawing of their daughter during the visit and she remained close to the family. Her cousin died unexpectedly of a stroke while Wang was on location, but she learned that Zhou Enlai and dozens of top Communist Party officials attended the funeral.[6] Zhou Enlai was to become very important in the future of the film industry during the Cultural Revolution. He was loved by the Chinese people for all of his contributions to the society.[7]

As the Great Leap Forward was coming to an end at the beginning of 1960, it had resulted in severe economic dislocations and food shortages. This, coupled with the withdrawal of the Soviet Union's technical assistance, as well as the need for liberalized economic policies, meant that a professionally oriented element was rising to power in China's political bureaucracy. And most of all, the previous restrictions on intellectual freedom were gradually being relaxed.[8]

Two years later, the Communist Party conference in Beijing denounced the Great Leap Forward with the majority of the delegates in agreement. Mao retained symbolic power, but lost his grip over the day-to-day management of economic policy.

During this period, Wang Renmei continued to experience mental problems and worked on and off again with the Beijing Film Studio. She was still concerned about her acting skills and attended a class which prepared students to pass the movie artist qualifications exam. As she studied the art of acting systematically, she became more passionate about the profession.[9]

Wang Renmei received a small part as a mother of the friend of Fang Xiaohua's mother in the film *Hua'er Duoduo* (*Flowers*), which was about children who want to celebrate various holidays and form a group. In this case, the children are waiting for a talented singer, Fang Xiaohua, who unfortunately shows up very late, and others have to improvise while waiting. The film, which was poorly made, only shows the singing festival which describes in song why Fang was late. Apparently, a horse cart was overturned on the road just as the train was about to come and hit it, causing a dangerous situation. Fang, not afraid, faced all sorts of obstacles and crossed a dangerous flowing river to get to the railroad tracks, stood on the tracks, waved his scarf as the train approached in order to avert a tragedy. The children, hearing the song, are overcome with emotion and everyone sings, "the flowers all face the sun" as the film ends.[10]

Wang was disappointed because her role was only seen in one or two scenes and she had no speaking parts. However, as a good team player, she continued to lobby to make more films and director Dong Kena invited her to play in what was to become her last film, *Kunlunshan Shang Yi Ke Cao* (*A Blade of Grass on Mount Kunlun*, a.k.a. *Grass on Mount Kunlun*). She appeared as the mother of Li Wanli during the struggle on Mount Kunlun. The film itself is a typical Communist propaganda piece showing how formerly inaccessible places could now be reached through hard work by members of the Communist Party. The final scene shows the heroine, Li Wanli, who has achieved the great height of Mount Kunlun, sitting on the grass shrouded in frost, with the sun shining forth with the promise of life. She makes a pledge and is willing to give her youth to the high plateau.[11]

Although Wang Renmei was disappointed with her lack of participation in these films except in tiny roles, she was responsible for the costumes and continuity on many of the productions of the Beijing Film Studio. So her work at the film company, although not as an actress, was as important to her in demonstrating her contribution to the entire company.

She was rewarded with roles in several plays put on by the acting troupe, including *The Army Approaching the City,* performed in 1962. Later that year, she became a member of the work team of the "four purges." This movement was aimed at purging the politics, the economy, the organization, as well as "old thoughts" in the countryside. She was sent to Shanxi Province with a group to assist in this project. When she returned to Beijing, she was accused of being "a black cat" in the 1930s. These accusations, calling her an anti-revolutionary, added to her mental instability.

The "four purges" movement was a forerunner to what happened in 1966 with the advent of the Cultural Revolution. Mao, whose power had been diminished a few years earlier, declared to himself "enough was enough." So, seventeen years after the liberation of China by the Communist Party, Mao firmly believed that his line of thought, especially in the field of culture, was not being carried out, and in fact had encountered stubborn resistance. He believed many in the party continued their futile and bourgeois ideology in the arts. An example was the Peking Opera's *Hai Rui Dismissed from Office*, written by Wu Han. That finally was the last straw for Mao. He said the play was a political dissertation against the party and socialism and "promoted feudal and capitalistic art." And he stated that similar ideas were reflected on the stage, screen, and in print. He therefore created the Great Proletarian Cultural Revolution to solve the question of ideology, which he believed was more important than the economic issues of the time.[12]

The Central Committee of the Communist Party met in Beijing and issued the following directive concerning the Cultural Revolution:

> At present, our objective is to struggle against and overthrow those persons in authority who are taking the capitalist road, to criticize and repudiate the reactionary bourgeois academic "authorities" and the ideology of the bourgeoisie and all other exploiting classes and to transform education, literature and art and all other parts of the superstructure not in correspondence with the socialist economic base, so as to facilitate the consolidation and development of the socialist system.[13]

Students and Red Guard units went on a spree, closing schools, attacking their teachers, and creating havoc around the country. Mao had asked all of the college students as well as the younger ones to participate, and millions of young people were mobilized to take part.[14]

Zhou Enlai, in September, had to admonish certain Red Guard units for going too far in the northern Chinese city of Harbin. He said their mistake was to attack the entire provincial party leadership as the "black gang" and said, "some of the provincial committee comrades are good, not all party organizations are bad."[15]

According to historian Richard Baum, the Cultural Revolution was Mao's way to "immunize the Chinese people against the pernicious virus of Khrushchev's apostate revisionism." It was apparent that there were major differences between the Soviet and the Chinese Communist Party leadership in how they approached the problems of economic and social development. The goal of the Russians was professionalism in their bureaucratic and operational expert hierarchies, especially in industry, state administration, and the military. The Chinese had a different view and had a distrust of vertically integrated bureaucracies, highly trained professionals, and economic specialists. The Chinese Communist Party "adopted a populist approach to social change which called for the horizontal integration of society on the basis of subjectivity and mobilized masses under the direct combat-style leadership of red cadres." Mao especially did not trust the Russians, and now Khrushchev. In fact, he learned that anti-Mao leaders in his own party had met with representatives of the Soviet Union.[16]

Two year later, Wang Renmei's husband, Ye Qianyu, was arrested and labeled as a Guomindang agent with the title of "Major General" and thrown in prison. The reason for this was that during the anti-Japanese war he could not make a living in Chongqing, so he drew propaganda paintings and cartoons for the Sino-American cooperation center, which was a front for the Guomindang intelligence. His Red Guards said that he was better paid than a "Major General," so they accused him of being a Guomindang "Major General." He remained in prison for seven years.

In 1975, Ye came out of prison and went back to the Central Art College where he was a janitor. The next year, he almost died of a heart attack, and in 1978 he had a major operation. During all of this time, Wang Renmei supported the family.

In 1973, Wang was sent down to the countryside "to receive education." When she arrived and started to register, her jailer told her that she was "liberated" and was allowed to go back to Beijing to receive medical treatment. Although she was surprised at this turn of events, Wang realized that it was Chairman Mao who enabled her to be released. In addition, her relatives were spared ill treatment during the Cultural Revolution, thanks to Chairman Mao.[17]

Although Wang returned to Beijing, she kept a low profile because Madame Mao, a former film actress in Shanghai, had proclaimed a cleansing of all Chinese arts, especially film, and purged the entire industry.[18]

In January of 1976, Zhou Enlai died. Millions of Chinese were bereft. Yuhua Dong, a student leader during the Cultural Revolution, recalled that people were very sad and seriously so. They believed that everything was going to collapse. Zhou was important to the country because everyone knew he was the one who held things together. "He was the force of stability. The students knew that Mao stood there, but everyone believed that he was up there with big ideas, causing all kinds of movement, but they also knew that Mao changed his mind a lot. Zhou, on the other hand, was very steady and was trusted by the people. They knew that he was the one that made sure everything was running in China and that the factories kept producing during the Cultural Revolution and that people had enough to eat. He was the one that made sure that everything was all right."[19]

A few months later, Mao died and again people were shocked. The population felt that China had lost its direction; they did not know where to go, and there was a general fear that there might be a kind of turmoil because of the chairman's death. "Mao had always been about where the movement would go. After his death, we didn't know where to go."[20]

With the deaths of both Zhou Enlai and Mao Zedong, the Chinese population was at a loss and the government seemed rudderless. At that moment, Deng Xiaoping and other Communist Party leaders who were ostracized by Mao at the start of the Cultural Revolution, returned to positions of power. Hua Guofeng, the successor to Chairman Mao, arrested the so-called Gang of Four, which included Madame Mao. Immediately, Wang Renmei regained her position with the Beijing Film Studio and received salary compensation for the entire period of the Cultural Revolution. She also attended the Fifth National Political Consultant Conference that was held shortly afterwards. On November 8, 1979, she was admitted as a member of the Communist Party in a ceremony at the Beijing Actors Troupe. It had been over twenty years since she first submitted her application in 1956 to join the Communist Party.

Wang believed this was the start of a new life for her. She wanted to explore a whole new field and to study to be a movie director because she had already started to direct a play, *Sunrise*, with Ba Hong in the fall of 1979. However, a few months later, she suffered from a brain blood thrombosis and became half paralyzed.[21]

It is ironic that with the incarceration of Madame Mao as one of the Gang of Four, which gave Wang Renmei an opportunity to regain her activities at the Beijing Film Studio, her illness forced her to retire. At the same time, production started again. The rightists were rehabilitated and restored to positions of influence, and with Deng re-established as a power behind the government; the mistakes made during the Cultural Revolution were recognized. The Beijing Film Academy was reopened.[22]

When Wang Renmei returned from the hospital, she was confined to a wheelchair and lived in a courtyard house with her husband, Ye Qianyu, who had been released from prison a few years before and now was back teaching in the national painting department of the Central Art College. He received compensation for his incarceration during the Cultural Revolution and his back salary. The sum of RMB 30,000 given to him was donated by Ye to the Central Art College for a scholarship fund for students.

Wang's husband continued to paint and sell his art works for large sums of money. However, the conditions under which they lived did not improve, since the painter did not know how to handle his financial gains and went through the income quickly. The house where they resided needed serious repair. The pipes leaked, the floors were rotten, and the front door could not be closed.

Wang Renmei urged Ye to appeal to the housing office in charge of maintenance several times, but he did not do so. He explained that the housing office had difficulty as well and that the rent was not even enough to repair the house. The painter told her that he was never worried by the trivial things in life, and one should appreciate what he or she had now to be happy. Wang Renmei realized how set in his thinking her husband was and thought once again she had married another stubborn man.[23]

During the time of her disability in Shanghai, she was interviewed by writer Xie Bo. Xie remarked that she had a problem moving around at home but did not want anyone to take care of her and only thought of looking after others. She noted that the heating system in her house was old and inefficient. But when Xie offered to ignite the furnace, she declined and said that she wanted to do it herself. "Then she tried to ignite a match and at the same time turn on the gas furnace. Then, there came the breathtaking scene. It was either she could not ignite the match, or the match flew out of her hand. But she never gave up, and tried one match after another. Finally, she got the fire. Throughout the process, she would not allow me to help."[24]

Xie observed that whenever she visited Wang Renmei, she was often interrupted by visitors. She had many friends, some from her days back in the Bright Moon Troupe, as well as actresses from the Beijing Film Studio. She showed her a doll that was not destroyed by the Red Guards during the Cultural Revolution. It was given to her by Wu Yonggang to console her for the loss of her child when she was married to Jin Yan. Wang had put a plastic cover on it and placed it on the top of a bookshelf. One of the people who came to visit her was the wife of the door guard of the Beijing Film Studio who had taken care of Wang Renmei when she was ill. To compensate for her kindness, the woman had been supported financially by Wang. She also supported her neighbors who had several children and were in dire need of funds. The writer was impressed with the positive attitude of Wang Renmei even though she was confined to her wheelchair.[25]

As her illness became worse in the mid-1980s, she was forced to stay in bed for long periods of time. She reviewed her whole life and believed that she became famous because of her courage and willingness to experiment and "rush forward." However, she was convinced that her misfortune was tied to her unwillingness to move on and expand. She believed that when one becomes famous, it probably is due to luck. She contemplated that had she not been a hardworking member of the Bright Moon Troupe and displayed courage when she first entered the movie industry, she would not have been so famous. But she lamented that she became famous at too young an age, and when applause and praise filled her ears, she forgot who she was. When she eventually realized the importance of studying the art of acting, it was already too late and she was already too old.[26]

Notes

1. Wang Renmei, *Memoir: Wo de chengming yu buxing*, p. 19.
2. Meyer, *Jin Yan*, p. 100.
3. *Encyclopedia of Chinese Films*, Volume 2, p. 923.
4. Ibid., pp. 765–766.
5. *The Song of Youth*, 35 mm film (Beijing: Chinese Film Archive).
6. Wang Renmei, *Memoir: Wo de chengming yu buxing*, pp. 17–19.

7. Interview, Yuhua Dong, June 12, 2011.
8. Richard Baum (ed.), *China in Ferment: Perspectives on the Cultural Revolution* (Englewood Cliffs, NJ: Prentice-Hall Inc., 1971), p. 9.
9. Wang Renmei, *Memoir: Wo de chengming yu buxing*, pp. 260–261.
10. *Encyclopedia of Chinese Films*, Volume 2, p. 388.
11. Ibid., p. 510.
12. Gerald Tannenbaum, "China's Cultural Revolution: Why It Had to Happen," in Richard Baum (ed.), *China in Ferment*, pp. 60–66.
13. "Decision of the Central Committee of the Chinese Communist Party Concerning the Great Proletarian Cultural Revolution," *Peking Review*, No. 33 (August 12, 1966), pp. 6–12.
14. Interview, Yuhua Dong, June 12, 2011.
15. Philip Bridgham, "Mao's Cultural Revolution: Origin and Development," (part 2), in Baum (ed.), *China in Ferment*, p. 118.
16. Richard Baum, "Ideology Redivivus," in Baum (ed.), *China in Ferment*, pp. 67–71.
17. Interview, Dr. Wang Yong, March 26, 2010.
18. Jay Leyda, *Dianying, Electric Shadows*, pp. 342–343.
19. Interview, Yuhua Dong, June 12, 2011.
20. Ibid.
21. Wang Renmei, *Memoir: Wo de chengming yu buxing*, p. 262.
22. Meyer *Jin Yan*, p. 112.
23. Wang Renmei, *Memoir: Wo de chengming yu buxing*, pp. 236–239.
24. Xie Bo, "Preface," in Wang Renmei, *Memoir: Wo de chengming yu buxing*, pp. 284–285.
25. Ibid., p. 289.
26. Wang Renmei, *Memoir: Wo de chengming yu buxing*, p. 262.

CHAPTER 7

Wang Renmei in the End

W ang Renmei was keenly aware of events taking place in China during the 1980s, even though she was ill. She was very impressed with the work of Deng Xiaoping, and how he had assisted those who had suffered, including himself, under the Cultural Revolution. He had to intervene numerous times to mend differences among the Communist Party leaders, and in the early 1980s, when he was looking for a viable blueprint for systematic institutional reform, he was compelled to "cross the river by groping for stepping stones." The paramount leader, as he was known, was improvising as he went along. He introduced a series of ad hoc piecemeal measures, designed to facilitate early change. Some examples were the establishment of the Central Advisory Committee (CAC) to move elderly party cadres aside so that younger leaders could have power. He also modernized and professionalized the People's Liberation Army, and created a two-tier price structure to help ease the transition to a market-related pricing system.[1]

Deng's method of removing older members from the governing body of the Communist Party, using the concept of "feudal influence," was organized so that no leading cadres could hold office indefinitely.

Deng, as an example, resigned as vice-premier, thereby forcing the resignations of Premier Hua Guofeng and 16 vice-premiers, making it possible to bring in fresh leadership. Wang Renmei was even able to vote in a local election for county-level officials, which was one of the reforms initiated by Deng.[2]

During her last days, Wang Renmei applauded the work of Deng Xiaoping and his associates, who were instrumental in removing 150,000 members from the Communist Party for corruption and other misdeeds.[3] Private enterprise under his leadership was encouraged even though it was opposed by the conservative elements in the Communist Party. Deng reorganized the People's Liberation Army by reducing the number of troops, thereby forcing the retirement of conservative generals and enabling the promotion of younger cadres in 1985.

On her deathbed, Wang Renmei was disheartened to hear about student protest movements on various campuses. In 1986, many of them wanted more democracy, and there were individual demonstrations in Beijing and Shanghai with crowds estimated to be around 30,000 people in each city. Deng blamed lax leadership for the student protests, and said that some of them should be expelled from the party. In a precursor to the Tiananmen Square massacre of 1989, he said a "show of force" was necessary to those who were determined to provoke a confrontation: "If they want to create a bloody incident, what can we do about it? . . . We do all we can to avoid bloodshed . . . If we do not take the appropriate steps and measures, we will be unable to control this type of incident; if we pull back, we will encounter even more trouble later on . . ."[4]

Wang Renmei agreed wholeheartedly with the action to suppress the students. She thought they were ungrateful because she lamented that the young people of today, living under the condition of socialism, had much better conditions than she had. She hoped that young people should not have to rely on their parents or expect luck. In order for them to fulfill their ambitions to have a successful career, they had to work hard and lay the foundation to gain real knowledge. The students, she observed, should be perseverant, experience hardship and get to know themselves while achieving even small goals. She worried that many of them were self-contented and as a consequence, would fall behind. In addition, she worried about the press coverage of young people who had not accomplished very much. She realized that praise should be no more and no less—just right—and should be combined with criticism. "That's true love for youth and the right way to encourage talented people."[5]

Wang Renmei's life was connected to the life and times of Mao Zedong. The chairman of the world's most populated country had been the student of Wang's father in Changsha and spent one summer living in the the Wangs' house when the actress was a child. Her story and her life reflected a turbulent time of China, from the end of the Qing dynasty to the rise of Deng Xiaoping. She was born in Hunan Province to a feudal family in 1914, the youngest of ten children and was spoiled by her older siblings. She was helped by them to receive an education after her father died. She became proficient in singing and dancing and was discovered by Li Jinhui, the father of Chinese popular music, who enrolled her in the Bright Moon Troupe. Touring southeast Asia with the group, she learned to perform in front of various audiences. Discovered by Sun Yu, the director at Lianhua Studios, she had a leading role in the film *Wild Rose* opposite her future husband, Jin Yan. Her debut was hailed by critics and audiences alike as the newest star in the Hollywood of Asia. She was on a fast track to becoming one of China's leading film stars. Yet, after her most famous film, *Song of the Fishermen*, in which she sang and played a major role, her career started to go downhill.

Her contract with the film studio was not renewed because the owner believed that a female who was married would no longer appeal to male audiences. She continued to make films but was not as successful as her husband, Jin Yan. After the Japanese occupation, she and Jin smuggled themselves out of Shanghai and went to Hong Kong. They were divorced at the end of World War II, after she had taken a job with the American forces in China as a typist, since her knowledge of English was excellent. That stint, as well as her entertaining Guomindang troops during World War II, had a dire effect on her career after the establishment of the People's Republic of China. Yet, she persevered and agreed to accept bit parts in films.

Wang Renmei continued to demonstrate her loyalty to the Chinese Communist Party and applied for membership. It took her over twenty years to achieve it because of many factors, one of which was her mental illness. During the Anti-Rightist Campaign, she was criticized and then during the Cultural Revolution, she was sent to a detention camp for re-education. Suddenly, she was liberated and allowed to return to Beijing to receive medical treatment. Later, she learned that Chairman Mao had interceded. Her second marriage to famous artist Ye Qianyu was stormy, and she continued to have mental problems. Her stroke and paralysis in 1980 cut short any hope she had of returning to any acting or directing role.

Although Wang Renmei appeared in 25 films, she lamented that she became famous at too young an age. At the end of her life, in December of 1987, she realized that she should have studied acting, but by the time she became a star, "it was already too late." Yet, today, her films are being discovered again.

Wang Renmei's life symbolized what thousands of artists of her time experienced as well. They desired to help the new China, but reactionary forces thwarted their chances. Only during the era of Deng Xiaoping did they get rehabilitated. Wang's illness prevented her from receiving the same treatment many of her colleagues received when they were able to return to their positions at the Beijing Film Studio. Wang Renmei, had she not gotten sick, could have been rehabilitated in Chinese cinema.

Wang Renmei's voice was known to anyone in the Chinese population who had a phonograph or listened to the radio. Her songs, many of which were from her motion pictures, were recorded with other popular songs of the day. One of the most famous musicologists in China, Dr. Wang Yong, stated that Wang Renmei was one of the great singers of the 1930s and expressed her songs with such emotion that she had an impact on her listeners. Actress Qin Yi believed that Wang's life was really one in which she should be pitied, even though she was a wonderful actress and extrovert.

One has to place Wang Renmei in the context of the horrible times in which she lived. It is obvious that she had raw talent, a beautiful voice, and a fabulous stage presence. She, like many of her contemporaries, could not overcome the effects of the Cultural Revolution even though they were given a second chance by Deng Xiaoping. She was more fortunate than some of her colleagues, who either were jailed for many years or committed suicide, because of her relationship with Mao Zedong. Her life, intertwined with the chairman of the Communist Party, could have been much worse. She was also fortunate to have a well-connected family who were active in the work of the Communist Party both in China and abroad.

Wang Renmei's downfall as a leading lady is not unusual in the annals of screen history. For example, Hollywood has had its share of leading ladies, such as Ruby Keeler, who were known for their singing and dancing, only to be forgotten as they aged. Many of them tried to resurrect their careers with dramatic roles, some with little success.

Wang Renmei may best be remembered for her extravagant behavior onscreen and her singing, but also her lasting claim to immortality is the film *Wild Rose*. If one were to encapsulate the life and times of Wang Renmei with one film, it has to be *Wild Rose*. On the screen, we see her in all of her vitality and "wildcat" spirit, fighting against all odds, making personal sacrifices and finally going to the aid of her nation.

Thanks to modern technology, the film has been restored and made available on DVD to audiences in China and many Western countries. In addition, her songs and film clips are available on the web. Just as Mao Zedong is being re-examined, so too is Wang Renmei's career whose life was related to that of the chairman.

Notes

1. Richard Baum, *Burying Mao: Chinese Politics in the Age of Deng Xiaoping* (Princeton, NJ: Princeton University Press, 1994), pp. 10–17.
2. Ibid., pp. 98–108.
3. Ibid., pp. 167–168.
4. Ibid., pp. 202–205.
5. Wang Renmei, *Memoir: Wo de chengming yu buxing*, pp. 262–263.

Interview with Qin Yi
July 4, 2009

Richard J. Meyer — RJM
Qin Yi — QY

RJM: I became very interested in Wang Renmei after we had that discussion in Shanghai.

Do you have any names and addresses of people who are still alive and knew Wang Renmei?

QY: She has no immediate family. She had a brother who played the violin but he passed away last year. Her brother might have children who may still be alive.

RJM: What is the name of the brother?

QY: Wang Renlu.

RJM: And he lived in Shanghai?

QY: Yes. Wang's other brother has also passed away recently. He lived in Shanghai. He might have had children, too.

    If the two brothers were still alive, they would be in their nineties, so their children are probably 50 or 60 years old.

RJM: I found out that her brothers paid for Wang's school tuition after her father died.

QY: Yes. Maybe it's that way.

RJM: Did you appear on screen with Wang Renmei?

QY: I made a film in 1951 with her and it was called *Liangjia Chun*.

RJM: How was it working with her? Could you describe some examples?

QY: I liked working with her because she really enjoyed it as she had a very outgoing personality. She was a real extrovert. She had a nickname. Her nickname was "wildcat." Before liberation, she made a whole bunch of films and she was really outgoing and exuberant and that was the reason why Jin Yan liked her—not because she was good-looking but because she had such a vibrant, outgoing, and enthusiastic personality.

    When we were shooting *Liangjia Chun*, actually Wang Renmei didn't have a lot of experience. I played the main role and Wang Renmei was just playing some young girl. Wang Renmei was so outgoing that whenever we had any free time, she would go to the countryside and buy the local goods that farmers were selling, such as liquor or chicken livers, and she would bring them back, give them to me and say, "Jin Yan likes these, take them back to him."

She would also buy flour from nearby farmers and they didn't have a lot to eat at that time, so whatever they had, she would put in flour and fry it with a little bit of sugar and then mix it up and it would be really good. One of the things that she cooked was beef bone marrow and she would fry it in flour and sugar and they thought it was great—it tasted really good.

At that time, Wang Renmei still regretted the divorce quite a bit and I would see her. It wasn't so much that she thought she was some great woman, she just felt bad about the divorce because Wang Renmei had a really bad temper. Once she started fighting with Jin Yan, she would just go off. She still felt bad about the situation. She was a little envious.

Later, the company in Shanghai transferred her to Beijing because her mood became so bad that she became very depressed. It was even worse than depression, so they sent her off to Beijing. If you don't want to, you don't need to write all of this. You can pick and choose because this is kind of an embarrassing thing.

I felt sorry for her and felt a lot of sympathy for her, but it was too late because I was already married to Jin Yan. There was nothing that I could do.

Wang Renmei herself was actually a very nice person. I was very good to her so she felt really bad about it.

Also, she didn't have any malice. She would bring something back and she would say, "Oh, take this back to Jin Yan." It was completely without malice. She just said, "He likes this, so take it back."

RJM: No jealousy?

QY: I was not jealous. She was just very open. She knew that this was an established fact and she hoped that we had a good relationship—a good marriage. But there was no way to get over her nostalgia for Jin Yan.

Everyone was really mature.

RJM: Did you associate socially, at any time, with Wang Renmei?

QY: In the course of making the film and working together, we did become very good friends. Later, when Wang Renmei wasn't being filmed anymore, very few people went to see her. I continued to visit her until she died. I was a fan of hers.

RJM: Was she at your wedding banquet with Jin Yan?

QY: No, we got married in Hong Kong and Wang wasn't in Hong Kong.

RJM: She wasn't there. Okay. I know a Madam X was there.

QY: The situation was this: at our wedding banquet in Hong Kong, this Madam X was actually a friend of Wang Renmei's and she came on her behalf. She started to talk to Jin Yan and started to revile him, "How could you ever get divorced with Wang Renmei? You shouldn't have done that." Madam X was saying that when she was sitting right next to him. Jin Yan thought it was a huge insult to his bride. The woman ran out. He was so mad. He got up and threw a chair. He was so mad. He was so angry. He went after her.

RJM: I know the story, then he ran after the tram and disappeared.

Did you ever meet Wang's second husband? If so, what was he like?

QY: Here's the story about the guy. His name is Ye Qianyu. Her second husband was originally an artist—he drew comics and cartoons for newspapers. He was first married to a ballerina but the ballerina ran off with another young ballet star and left him alone. Then he started to pay court to Wang Renmei and he got her. They got married but he always remembered, missed, and thought about his former wife, the ballerina. He didn't treat Wang Renmei very well. He was always trying to paint or do his comics. The way Wang Renmei was—anytime something came up, she would want to come in and talk to him. She had a very extroverted, outgoing personality. She would want to come in and tell him everything. He didn't pay any attention to her. It finally got to a point where he didn't even want to talk to her. When Madam X and her friends visited Wang Renmei, he wouldn't even come out. He would stay in the back.

When Wang Renmei got sick and was near death in the hospital, he wouldn't even go to the hospital. After she died, he didn't go to the funeral.

RJM: Not a good guy.

QY: She also felt he was cruel-hearted.

RJM: Did they get divorced, officially?

QY: They didn't get divorced. He got divorced with his first wife, the ballerina. But the first wife ran away, ran off.

RJM: Now, your film career is still going on—it still continues, but Wang Renmei's career ended many years before she died. What happened?

QY: She got sick after 1951. So then she was sent to the Beijing Studio.

RJM: Now this is a delicate question.

QY: No problem.

RJM: I read that Wang Renmei was involved in several groups criticizing certain artists and officials. I don't know if it was during the Cultural Revolution or before, but she was very active in these groups. I can't remember the exact names but they were criticizing certain individuals. Do you have any recollection of that kind?

QY: The only thing I know is that during the War of Resistance, Wang Renmei worked for the Americans as a typist. Jin Yan didn't agree with that.

During the Cultural Revolution, I really don't know but she was already sick. I think she had a mental breakdown.

RJM: Yes. Right.

QY: During the Cultural Revolution, she was sick and she also hadn't made as many films as she had before. She wasn't like some big famous person, so she had much less trouble during the Cultural Revolution than they did. But she didn't have—it's not like she had—a great time.

Her husband was attacked because he was famous.

RJM: So he got into trouble.

QY: Yes.

RJM: I only have two more questions.

It took Wang Renmei a very long time to become a party member and I know that you were accepted very, very soon. Why do you think it was difficult for Wang Renmei to join the party? I think it took her twenty years or so.

QY: I don't know specifically, but it wasn't like that. It was more like, she got sick in 1951. If you are going to be a party member, you can't—they would take that into consideration. If you are a party member and you start saying anything randomly, it's not good. That's why.

Probably what happened is that they did consider, but then later, in order to honor her movies or something—they let her do it.

Here's something I bet you didn't know . . .

RJM: What?

QY: Wang Renmei had no political problems because her father was a teacher of Chairman Mao's.

RJM: I knew that when she was a little girl, Mao spent the summer at her house.

QY: She was in the northeast at this time, but when Wang Renmei was a little kid, Chairman Mao went to her father's house. She heard that when he got there, the first thing he said was, "Where's Renmei?" She was just a little kid. Normally, he didn't pay much attention to young actors or actresses, but because her father was his teacher, he knew her and so he was interested.

I think that is probably why during the Cultural Revolution, she didn't have any problems.

RJM: How would you describe her as a human being and as an actress?

QY: In terms of a person, she really had a good heart. She was a really good person. She was very exuberant and outgoing. Whether it was in the old days or in the movie circles, she was always making a lot of friends. She was always extremely outgoing and talking to people, making a lot of friends. Later, she got sick. Even after she got sick in 1951, she was still able to do some work.

I asked about what kinds of symptoms she had when she got ill, she said that she would do things like if she was feeling very sentimental, she would look at the moon when it was full and say, "Look, the moon is full. When am I ever going to have my reunion or fullness?" And that meant coming together with her family again, as well as with her husband. What she said was that she was a very sentimental and nostalgic person. She never got over Jin Yan. If she and the painter hadn't gotten married, then it's very likely that Wang Renmei and Jin Yan would have gotten together again. It's just because they got married. Otherwise, that might have happened.

If she was healthy, when I was standing next to her, she wouldn't say things out loud, like "how round the moon is" and "when am I ever going to get back together." If she had been healthy, she wouldn't have said that when I was standing next to her. She would say stuff like that and even when other people were around. She just wasn't normal at that time.

She was in a hospital in Beijing at that time so she wasn't able to work that much.

RJM: If you had to sum up Wang Renmei's life in a sentence or two, what would you say?

QY: It's a pity. It's a shame. I said earlier that she is someone to be pitied.

RJM: Her life is a pity or she's to be pitied?

QY: She's to be pitied.

She said that if they hadn't gotten divorced, maybe they could have continued to work together, continued to live together and it would have been okay.

RJM: You don't think her illness was precipitated by her divorce from Jin Yan.

QY: That's what she thinks. She said that she always felt that she could never get back together with him and that precipitated her illness.

RJM: I remember you told me in Shanghai that you told Jin that if he wanted to get back together with Wang Renmei, then please go ahead, and he got very angry.

QY: I knew he wouldn't be willing to do that.

Jin Yan said that based on their two personalities, even if they had gotten back together, they would have fought. They both had strong personalities.

The way Wang Renmei was, she would put her cup here and if somebody moved it, she would move it back. She said that Jin Yan was the same.

RJM: I can't imagine if they had the same cup!

QY: That's why they were constantly fighting.

RJM: I really appreciated your taking the time to talk with me.

QY: I was happy to help you.

Interview with Dr. Wang Yong
March 26, 2010

RJM–Richard J. Meyer
WY–Wang Yong

RJM: Dr. Wang, I appreciate that you had time to grant me an interview.

WY: Here is a book about my grandfather, Wang Renyi. My grandfather was Renmei's older brother. He was four years older than she.

RJM: Who wrote this book?

WY: I did.

RJM: You are a famous Shanghai musician and professor. Was your father also a musician?

WY: Yes.

RJM: Your father's father was the brother of Wang Renmei?

WY: No.

RJM: I don't understand.

WY: I called Renyi "grandfather." However, my father was his stepson.

RJM: Okay. So in reality, he was your step-grandfather?

WY: Yes.

RJM: As far as you were concerned, he was like a real grandfather?

WY: Yes. Because I was born in his family.

RJM: Right. So you were treated just like a grandson.

WY: Yes.

RJM: How old were you when your grandfather died?

WY: Fourteen.

RJM: So he died two years before his sister did?

WY: Yes.

RJM: How did you know how many years older he was than his sister?

WY: Wang Renyi was born in 1912. Wang Renmei was born in 1916, I think.

RJM: So there was a four-year difference? Now, since you were 14, did you see your grandfather often? Did he live in Shanghai?

WY: Yes. Yes.

RJM: Did he tell you any stories about his sister, Wang Renmei? Did he tell you anything about her?

WY: This is a long, long story.

RJM: Well, if you don't mind, I would like to hear it. So he talked about her?

WY: He talked about her. I remember one month they wrote letters to each other. He was able to discuss very important things with her.

          After Renyi passed away, Wang Renmei knew that his widow had no job and no income, so she helped. She put in her will that almost half of her assets would go to her brother's wife after her death.

RJM: And your grandmother was helped financially by Renmei?

WY: Yes.

RJM: Did your grandfather tell you any stories about Renmei?

WY: Their names: "Mei" means beauty; "Yi" is loyalty.

RJM: Their father was a very famous teacher and one of his students was Mao. You knew that?

WY: Yes.

RJM: Did your grandfather tell you any stories about Mao when he lived in the Wangs' house, since he was older and could observe when Renmei was very little. Did he remember Mao playing with her on his knees? Her brother must have been about six or seven years old. He must remember that because nobody knew at that time that Mao was going to be chairman. What did your grandfather have to say?

WY: He never mentioned anything between his father and Mao for a long time. He didn't discuss the relationship between his father as a teacher and Mao. During the revolution, Wang Renyi was himself, at that time, identified as a leftist.

The reason he didn't want to talk about it was that during the revolution, he was already viewed suspiciously and identified as the "left side." He was worried, if he was telling people about the relationship between Mao and himself, it might affect Chairman Mao as well.

I'm sure the people knew the truth about how the revolution was causing problems. In the middle of the revolution, the people in charge of the revolution were investigating the relationship between Wang Renyi and Chairman Mao. Wang Renyi asked his colleagues and/or students if he should tell the bureau about his relationship with Chairman Mao. Most of them recommended that he tell the truth.

RJM: When you say "revolution," you are talking about the Cultural Revolution, is that correct?

WY: Yes.

After he told the truth about his relationship with Chairman Mao, his identity got released in two or three months. At that time, the close relatives knew that the relationship between Chairman Mao and Wang Renyi was made public.

There was one more thing they found out during the Cultural Revolution concerning Wang Renyi's older sister, because her age was closer to Chairman Mao's. She had more in common with Mao than Wang Renyi.

At that time, Wang Renyi's older sister became very sick and was put in a really bad hospital.

Chairman Mao was informed about it, so he actually sent documents to the local Shanghai government telling them to improve the condition of the hospital for Wang's older sister. Then the older sister was transferred to the military hospital, which had better conditions; it was the hospital in Shanghai which only provided service for government officials.

Most of the crew in the hospital didn't know the relationship between Chairman Mao and the older sister. They sneaked around, asking people what the relationship was; how could a normal, ordinary patient come to this particular hospital to receive treatment?

After she passed away in that hospital, the relatives asked them how much they had to pay for the fees and everything, but the hospital told them that it was paid by the government. They didn't have to spend a cent.

Even after the Cultural Revolution, the Wang family still avoided speaking about their relationship with Chairman Mao, but during the Cultural Revolution, because of the relationship, they were helped by Chairman Mao.

RJM: You probably know that the younger sister, Renmei, was sent down during the Cultural Revolution, but as soon as she got there they said, "Oh no . . . you're free to go." She knew why but didn't say anything. She knew how it all worked out.

That is what they call serendipity—the luck! The fact that Chairman Mao was a student in the house of their father's. Little did they know, years later, that would be a blessing.

Do you remember anything else that your grandfather would say about his sister? Did he ever mention the illness of his younger sister, Renmei?

WY: My grandpa, as Renmei's older brother, had contact through letters. I only got information sometimes from my grandfather. At that time, they were just worried because Renmei couldn't take care of herself. She wasn't that independent.

Sometimes, Renmei's nephew or niece would pass by Shanghai to see us and tell us how she was doing in Beijing. The niece or nephew would call Renmei "Auntie."

At that time, the only things that they would say was that Wang Renmei was stubborn—stubborn and tried to be independent. They all tried to convince Renmei to have a nanny to look after her, but Renmei didn't want to have one. She had always lived by herself.

RJM: This is very useful information. I appreciate it very much.

I have some more questions. Did your father or step-grandfather ever tell you anything or any stories about Wang Renmei?

WY: As a matter of fact, I was born in 1969 in Shanghai. During the 1950s and 1960s, after Wang Renmei had gone to Beijing for her career, I actually only had contact with her a few times each year. My father couldn't know a lot of information about her as he only learned the information by letters.

RJM: So not really much to tell about that?

WY: No.

RJM: Have you seen any of Wang Renmei's films?

WY: I watched the film about fishermen. It's a silent film but with music in it.

RJM: Oh, *Song of the Fishermen*. That film was the first Chinese film to win an International award at the Moscow Film Festival. She sings in that film.

How old were you when you saw that film?

WY: About twenty-something.

Now with my research, it's very important to learn about Shanghai's music scene.

RJM: You know, of course, Wang Renmei started out as a singer with the Bright Moon Troupe. Could you give me your own personal impression of her performance in *Song of the Fishermen* and what you thought of the film?

WY: My opinion of the movie that was called the *Song of the Fishermen*—I was watching it as a researcher instead of a relative, because I was researching old Chinese pop songs.

RJM: I understand, but what was your impression, not as a relative but as a researcher? The sound, I know, is not good quality but for example, what was your impression of the way she sings or maybe the music?

WY: The first time I saw *Song of the Fishermen* (the remake), I was listening to some other singers' interpretations of the song. Because I was a researcher, I went back to the original singer. Then I saw Wang Renmei. I knew that Wang Renmei sang with quality in her voice. I could tell the difference between the singer now and Wang Renmei, how nicely she sang. That's my impression.

I discovered that Wang Renmei, as a singer, had great feelings.

The difference between the singers who sing "Song of the Fishermen" nowadays tend to focus on the technical part instead of the emotional part, but Wang Renmei focused on the emotional part.

RJM: In other words, what you found in the way she sang is that you feel the emotion of the words and the music. Is that fair?

WY: She's not only using emotion to sing the song, but she's also making a connection between the movie and the song together.

RJM: Because she's an actress?

WY: Yes.

RJM: Since you know the story, she related to the poor fishermen about whom the film was made. In other words, she observed the real fishermen when she was making the film, so that enabled her to express those emotions.

WY: So Wang Renmei was a director, too?

RJM: No. Wang Renmei observed real fishermen.

WY: She went to the fishermen's village?

RJM: Right. So, did you feel, as a musician, that she conveyed the sentiment of those fishermen and the life they had to lead?

WY: It's a bit hard to answer because I studied the songs that Wang Renmei sang in the movies. I think that she qualified as a professional singer at that time because she could choose a way that enabled her to express each line of each song with the music—I think this was why other people thought that she sang the song in *Song of the Fishermen* with emotion from the heart. I think, particularly for that song, she actually chanted as she prepared to sing the song.

RJM: From a professional point of view, is this how a professional musician would approach a song?

WY: Yes.

RJM: Did you listen to the other songs that she sang?

WY: Yes.

RJM: Were you able to see any of her other films that she made when sound came in where she sang? She made many films after that.

WY: Yes.

RJM: So you have seen the other films in which she sang?

WY: Yes.

RJM: Again, what, as a musician (not as a relative), did you think of the way she sang in those other films?

WY: I heard almost every single song of Wang Renmei's from 1931 to 1947.

She got better every time in her 16-year singing career.

RJM: So she improved the way she sang with each film—you could see improvement.

WY: Yes. I watched about four or five of her films, but I listened to all of her songs.

RJM: When you listened, what did you notice as she got older, as she got more mature?

WY: Technically, you can see she improved as she got older and she had greater breath control. She probably talked to other singers about ways to improve.

RJM: Did she have lessons? Did she study music and singing?

WY: Not really in the professional sense, during that time. In the old days most singers talked to each other about their experiences and exchanged information.

RJM: Is there anything else that you would like to say about your looking at her films or listening to her?

WY: All I can say is back in the old days, most of the movies presented songs as part of the movie.

RJM: Right. Sort of like Bollywood?

WY: Comparing her movie songs and her recordings, I find that Wang Renmei actually put more emotion into the movie songs than into her recordings. She was more emotional when singing the songs in her movies.

RJM: In other words, if she was just singing—not in a movie—she wasn't as emotional as in her movies.

WY: Yes.

RJM: Did she make any records?

WY: Yes.

RJM: Have you heard them?

WY: Yes.

RJM: Do you remember meeting Wang Renmei?

WY: Yes. I was young, and my impression was that she was a "superstar" but very friendly and a traditional "grandma." She was 70 years old at the time and looked like an old woman.

RJM: What are your final thoughts about Wang Renmei?

WY: According to my relatives, she was stubborn. Although I saw her infrequently, I found her to be a real professional.

RJM: Thank you very much for speaking with me today, Dr. Wang.

WY: It was my pleasure.

Interview with Yuhua Dong
June 12, 2011

RJM–Richard J. Meyer
YD–Yuhua Dong

RJM: How long have you lived in Beijing?

YD: 16 years.

RJM: And where did you move from?

YD: Hohhot, Mongolia.

RJM: How long did you live in Hohhot?

YD: Thirty-one years, since birth in 1945.

RJM: What is your overall opinion of Zhou Enlai?

YD: Since I was a kid and began to know things, I have always known him as our premier. We always thought of him as the most important statesman, only next to Mao. At the time, he was also the foreign minister. He always represented China to greet and receive foreign visitors, or to visit other countries. He was our icon.

RJM: What was his role during the Cultural Revolution?

YD: He played a very important role during the Cultural Revolution. One can say that without him, the Cultural Revolution wouldn't have developed the way it did.

RJM: Could you explain, when you say how it couldn't have developed the way it did?

YD: Not that he was leading the revolution but rather, during the revolution, he was the one who was holding the country up, making sure it was still running.

RJM: During the Cultural Revolution, what were you doing?

YD: At the beginning of the Cultural Revolution, I was in my second year, sophomore year, at college.

At that time, Mao asked all of the college students to participate in the Cultural Revolution and published a poster by a student from Peking University. That mobilized a lot of college students to participate. I became part of that movement. I participated in it.

RJM: Do you remember what year that was?

YD: That was June 3, 1966.

RJM: What did you do as a participating student?

YD: We wrote our own posters and a group of us met to discuss whether our party secretary carried out the policy in the right way or not.

RJM: What was your conclusion?

YD: The conclusion was that the party secretary's understanding of Mao's policy was wrong.

RJM: What happened to him?

YD: At the time, there was already a faculty member who was critical of the party secretary. So the student body also split into two camps.

RJM: You changed your position several times after college. Was it considered typical of the average person in China at that time?

YD: It was not very typical.

RJM: Then you feel that the average person got one job and stuck with that job for his whole career?

YD: Yes. Most people stuck with one job and did it for their whole life.

RJM: Even though they had to go through the Cultural Revolution.

YD: Yes.

RJM: As I understand it, you were at the factory when Zhou died.

YD: Yes. That is correct.

RJM: Do you recall what your reaction was and what the reactions of your fellow workers were, when he died?

YD: People were very sad and seriously so. The feeling was that everything was going to collapse. Zhou was so important because everyone knew that he was the one who held up the country. He was the force of stability. Mao stood there but everyone knew that Mao was up there with big ideas, causing all kinds of movement. Mao changed all of the time. Zhou was very steady and the people trusted him. They knew that he was the one who made sure everything was running. He made sure the farmers kept producing and that people had enough to eat. He was the one who made sure that everything was alright.

RJM: Well then, a few months later, Mao died. What was your reaction, as well as your fellow workers', to that?

YD: After Mao's death, people felt that China lost its direction. People didn't know where to go. There was a general fear that there might be some kind of turmoil because of his death. Mao had always been about the "where to go" movement. After his death, we didn't know where to go.

RJM: Do you think that the prosecution of the Gang of Four had anything to do with trying to create stability?

YD: Yes.

RJM: Who was the power behind the prosecution of the Gang of Four?

YD: The decision makers in the central government. Ming Li was chairman then, after Mao's death, and he was also a general. A wise party secretary and also one of the military generals—Wang Dongshi—was the head of the Central Police. This was the central government level.

At the local level, people were tired. They sensed that the Gang of Four were counterproductive.

RJM: Then you had the era of Deng Xiaoping. By this time, I think you were teaching chemistry. What were your reactions, as well as your fellow teachers' reactions, to the comeback of Deng?

YD: Generally, people thought that he was a very capable man. They all thought his comeback would help stabilize the country and help resume production.

RJM: What was the result of Deng coming back?

YD: Generally, he gave the country a direction. The direction led the country to prosperity. On the other hand, there might have been things that he couldn't foresee. For example, like we see now, with the corruption and the polarization of the rich and poor, and the social instability that comes with that. So he also led the country to a different direction and a different outlook. The country now had two sides: prosperity and a different kind of instability.

RJM: During this period, from the time you were in college to the time you became an editor, were you interested in going to the movies?

YD: Yes, I did. I liked going to the movies, especially during college. Movies were almost the only form of entertainment for people.

RJM: Do you remember any of the films that you saw in the early days?

YD: The earliest ones I can recall were those I saw during elementary school. Those films were mostly about war. The war films I saw were about the Korean War, such as one called *Shangaling,* and also a film about a white-haired girl that is about oppression, some espionage films; also some animation films made for kids. I also remember seeing Soviet films, for example, a story about World War II in the Soviet Union, and another one named *How Steel Was Made*.

A lot of anti-Japanese war films as well.

RJM: It's generally attributed to Zhou that he protected many people in the film industry during the height of the Cultural Revolution. What has been your experience with that?

YD: Zhou protected a lot of filmmakers. Filmmakers were among the first to be attacked during the Cultural Revolution largely because Madame Mao was in the film industry in the 1930s and a lot of the filmmakers knew her back then. They were perhaps more prominent at the time and she was not so much of a celebrity then. She had a grudge against them. Madame Mao made it the case that the film industry was under attack. Filmmakers were a major task for Zhou to protect.

RJM: Do you have any idea how—did people talk about how he protected not only the film industry, but other intellectuals and artists as well?

YD: At the beginning of the Cultural Revolution, Zhou was also at a loss. He didn't know what to do. Then, terrible things happened, like some of the intellectuals or cultural workers got harsh treatment. They were either beaten to death or they committed suicide. A lot of terrible things happened and these events alerted Zhou to do something. What he did was that he actually came up with a list of people to protect. He made sure that the people were treated well or that they were sent to a place where they were isolated and protected.

RJM: I think this gives me some insight into Zhou and before we end the interview, I would like to ask if you have any final thoughts or comments.

YD: I actually met with him in person for several times. I had close contact. I reported to him face-to-face. All together I met him three times.

RJM: In your role as part of the Student Revolutionary Committee?

YD: Not even that, it was before I was a committee member. That was when the Cultural Revolution was at its height. I met with him closely in February 1967. It was when the revolutionary situation got really complicated in Mongolia. Some big problems came up.

RJM: Do you have any other comments?

YD: Because of the big problem in Mongolia, the central government decided to send representatives from the military, from the party, and from the people, who had two points of view.

That just shows how diplomatic Zhou was. Basically, at the time, the party had a major conflict with the military, and they had problems with each other. Zhou, in a meeting with them, asked the representatives to try to calm down because the military was necessary to protect the country and the people. He suggested negotiating and mediating the conflict.

The meeting started at about 10 p.m. and didn't end until 2 a.m.

Zhou looked very tired. The secretary brought him a wet towel and then he continued to listen to reports from different parties. A lot of people talked to him — all four parties had five representatives each. There were 20 people in the room.

This is just another example of what a great man he was. He always cared about people. There was another time when I saw him in person in 1969. It was a much bigger conference. There were a lot of people. There was one of the four members there. Two military officials were criticized publically by the four. They were standing up. After they were criticized, they were never asked to sit down. Hours passed and they were still standing there. My dad in the audience was thinking how terrible it was. Zhou finally turned his head and gestured the two people to sit. For people in the audience, that really was a moment when they felt that Zhou was a benevolent person. He wanted to make people feel more comfortable.

RJM: Thank you for your time.

YD: Please don't mention it.

Filmography of Wang Renmei 1914–1987

Yinhe Shuangxing (*Double Stars Shining in the Milky Way/Two Stars Shining in the Milky Way*), 1931 Lianhua Studios, black and white; no sound; Director: Shi Dongshan; Cast: Wang Renmei, Jin Yan (Yang Yiyun), Zi Luolan (Li Yueying), Gao Zhanfei (Gao Qi), Ye Juanjuan, Chen Yanyan (actor), Song Weisai (Li Xudong), Li Jiqun (assistant director), Wang Cilong, Zhou Wenzhu, Sun Yu, Tang Tianxiu, Cai Chusheng, Li Lili, Zhou Ke, Dong Shaofen.

Bajiaoye Shang Shi (*Poetry on Palm Leaves*), 1931, Tian Yi Movie Company, black and white; Director: Sun Yu; Sound: Situ Huimin; Cast: Wang Renmei, Bright Moon Troupe.

Chunchao (*Stirring of Love/The Spring Tide*), 1931 Heng Sheng Film Company; Director: Zheng Yingshi; Script: Cai Chusheng; Cinematography: Chen Emian; Art: Cai Chusheng; Cast: Wang Renmei, Gao Zhanfei, Yuan Congmei.

Ye Meigui (*Wild Rose*), 1932 Lianhua Studios, black and white; no sound; Director: Sun Yu; Cast: Wang Renmei (Xiao Feng), Jin Yan (Jiang Bo), Ye Juanjuan (Su Qiu), Zheng Junli (Xiao Li), Wei Langen (Lao Qiang), Zhang Zhizhi (father of Xiao Feng), Hong Jingling (Hu Jin), Liu Jiqun (Lao Niu).

Gongfu Guonan (*Going to Aid the Nation Together/Coming to the Rescue of Our Country*), 1932, Lianhua Studios, black and white; Directors: Cai Chusheng, Shi Dongshan, Sun Yu, Wang Cilong; Script: Sun Ya; Cast: Wang Renmei (civilian), Jin Yan (volunteer soldier), Wang Cilong (Hua Weng), Gao Zhanfei (Zhangzi/eldest son), Song Wei (Cizi/second eldest), Deng Junli (Sanzi/third son), Jiang Junchao (Sizi /fourth son), Zhou Wenshu (Zhangxi/eldest daughter-in-law), Ye Juanjuan (Cixi/second daughter-in-law), Chen Yanyan (Zhangnu/eldest daughter), Liu Jiqun (servant).

Duhui De Zaochen (*The Morning of a Metropolis*), 1933, Lianhua Studios, silent; Director: Cai Chusheng; Cinematographer: Zhou Ke; Cast: Wang Renmei (Xu Lan'er), Gao Zhanfei (Xu Qiling), Yuan Congmei (Xu Huiling), Tang Huaiqiu (Huang Menghua), Wang Guiling (Xu Ada), Liu Jiqun (Xiao Zhang), Ye Juanjuan (a girl who loses her footing), Tang Tianxiu (Mr. Huang's wife), Han Langen (the youngest son).

Yu Guang Qu (*Song of the Fishermen*), 1934, Lianhua Studios, black and white; Director: Cai Chusheng; Cast: Wang Renmei (Xu Xiaomao), Luo Peng (He Ziying), Yuan Congmei (He Renzhai), Han Langen (Xu Xiaohou), Tan Ying (Xue Qiyun); Tang Guanwu (He Shunwen), Pei Yiwei (uncle).

Xiao Tianshi (*Little Angel*), 1934, Shanghai Film Studio, black and white, sound; Director: Wu Yonggang; Cast: Wang Renmei.

Fengyun Ernu (*Sons and Daughters of Wind and Cloud/Children of Troubled Times*), 1935, Diantong Film Company; Director: Xu Xingzhi; Scriptwriters: Tian Han, Xia Yan; Cinematography: Wu Yinxian; Cast: Wang Renmei (Ah Feng), Yuan Muzhi (Xin Baihua), Tan Ying (Madam Shi), Gu Menghe (Liang Zhifu), Lu Luming (girlfriend).

Changhen Ge (*The Song of Perpetual Regret*), 1936, Xinhua Enterprises; Director: Shi Dongshan; Cinematography: Cui Baoqing; Cast: Wang Renmei (Ma Nina), Mei Xi (Zhu Dongxin), Jin Shan (Hong Nanping), Wang Naidong (Xu Peilan), Gu Eri (Father Ma), Xu Manli (Yu Wanfen).

Zhuangzhi Lingyun (*Soaring Aspirations*), 1936, Xinhua Enterprises, black and white, sound; Director: Wu Yonggang, Cast: Wang Renmei (Black Clown), Jin Yan (Shun'er), Tian Fang (Tian Dehou), Zong You (Old Wang), Wang Cilong (Jian Xi), Han Langen (Monkey), Zhang Zhizhi (Fatty), Chen Juanjuan (Black Clown as a child), Jin Lun (Shun'er as a child).

Huanghai Dadao (*Pirates of the Yellow Sea*), 1937, Xinhua Enterprises; Script/Director: Wu Yonggang; Cast: Wang Renmei (Lin Qing), Chen Tianyuan (Liang Yongnian), Zhang Huiling (Lin Lushi), Gao Zhanfei (Zhang Zhong), Xu Mianwen (Wang Keqiao), Tang Jian (Director Zhao).

Li Hen Tian (*Parting from Heaven with Sorrow*), 1938, Xinhua Enterprises; Director: Wu Yonggang; Cinematography: Bi Boqing; Cast: Wang Renmei (Rose), Liu Qiang (Ah Bing Cheng), Bai Hong (Little Rose), Han Langen (Ah Gen), Yin Xiucen (Old Sheng), Zhang Zhizhi (Old Zhang).

Changkong Wanli (*Ten Thousand Mile Sky/Wings of China*), 1940, Zhongyang Movie Studios; Director: Sun Yu; Cinematography: Hong Weilie; Cast: Wang Renmei (Bai Yanxiu), Gao Zhanfei (Gao Fei), Bai Yang (Bai Feng), Jin Yan (Jin Wanli), Wei Heling (Le Yiqin), Shi Chao (Mr. Shi), Gu Eryi (Mr. Gu).

Chun Hui Dadi (*Spring Returning to the Earth*), 1941, Hong Kong; Cast: Wang Renmei (*never completed due to outbreak of World War II).

Jinxiu Jiangshan (*Beautiful Rivers and Mountains*), 1946, Suzhou; Cast: Wang Renmei (*never completed due to outbreak of Chinese Civil War).

Guanbuzhu De Chunguang (*Boundless Spring/The Spring That Cannot Be Confined*), 1948, Kunlun Movie Company; Director: Wang Weiyi; Script: Ouyang Yuqian; Cinematography: Wu Weiyun; Cast: Wang Renmei (Mei Chunli), Feng Zi (Mei Chunhua), Zhao Dan (Wu Jingzhi), Zhong Shuhuang (Chen Wenqi).

Wangshi Sixia (*Four Knight-Errants Named Wang*), 1949, Hong Kong Great Wall Film Company, black and white, sound; Director: Shi Dongshan; Cinematography: Zhou Shimu; Cast: Wang Renmei (extra), Wang Yuanlong (Older Brother Wang),

Wang Xuefei (Wang Changyun), Wang Yingzhi (Wang Shidong), Wang Zhengxin (Wang Yizai), Wang Naidong (Wang Wulao), Zhou Wenzhu (Wang Yizai's daughter), Xie Yunqing (the brigand chief).

Liangjia Chun (*The Double Spring/A Spring for Two Families*), 1951, Changjiang Movie Production Company; Director: Qu Baiyin; Script: Li Hongxin (based on the novel, *Breaking Apart the Bitter Melon*); Cinematography: Shi Fengzhi; Cast: Wang Renmei (head of the women's ward), Qin Yi (Zhui'er), Gao Bo (Da Kang), Wang Longji (Xiao Yong).

Menghe De Liming (*The Dawn of River Meng/Dawn over River Meng*), 1955, Changchun Film Studio; Directors: Lu Ren, Zhu Danxi; Screenplay: Zhu Danxi, Sun Mu, Shi Chao; Cinematography: Li Guanghui; Art: Wang Guiji; Music: Chang Lemin, Liu Wenpu; Cast: Wang Renmei (extra), Zhu Danxi (Luobu Danzeng), Tao Peng (Da Erjie), Su Man (Xie Chunbu), Liu Ru (Lang Jie), Liu Dachi (Chen Shaohua), Ba Lihua (Huang Hanchu).

Qingchun De Jiaobu (*The Steps of Youth*), 1957, Changchun Film Studio; Director: Su Li; Script: Xue Yandong; Cinematography: Li Guanghui; Art: Tong Jingwen; Music: Quan Rufen; Cast: Wang Renmei (Shufang), Yuan Mei (Lin Meilan), Chen Ying (Peng Ke), Liu Zengqing (Xiao Ping).

Tanqin Ji (*The Story of Visiting Family/Story of Visiting Relatives*), 1958, Beijing Film Studio; Script: Yang Runshen; Director: Xie Tian; Cinematography: Gao Hongtao, Chen Guoliang; Art: Tian Shizhen, Zhang Xiande; Music: Shi Lemeng; Cast: Wang

Renmei (extra), Wei Heling (Tian Laogeng), Zhang Yuan (Zhao Yushu), Zhang Ping (the third son), Sang Fu (Tian Gang).

Qingchun Zhi Ge (*The Song of Youth*), 1959, Beijing Film Studio; Director: Cui Wei; Script: Yang Mo; Art: Qin Wei; Music: Luo Bujian; Cast: Wang Renmei (mother of Lin Daojing's friend), Xie Fang (Lin Daojing), Yu Yang (Jiang Hua), Yu Shizhi (Yu Yongze), Qin Wen (Wang Xiaoyan), Ma Chenxi (Bai Liping), Kang Qin (Lu Jiachuan), Qin Yi (Lin Hong), Zhao Lian (Dai Yu), Zhang Miansheng (Hu Luoan).

Hua'er Duoduo (*Flowers*), 1962, Beijing Film Studio; Directors: Xie Tian, Chen Fangqian; Script: Xie Tian, Chen Fangqian; Cinematography: Li Wenhua, Chen Guoliang; Art: Xiao Bin, Mo Renji; Music: Kang He, Ding Ping; Cast: Wang Renmei (Fang Xiaohua's mother), Liu Jin (Fang Xiaohua), Cao Zengyin (old caretaker), Zhang Shipeng (little backstage manager), Hu Zhongtao (little assistant manager).

Kunlunshan Shang Yi Ke Cao (*A Blade of Grass on Mount Kunlun/ Grass on Mount Kunlun*), 1962, Beijing Film Studio; Director: Dong Kena; Script: Hua Ming, Dong Kena (based on the novel, *Hui Sao*); Cinematography: Gao Hongshou; Art: Zhang Xiande; Music: Liu Zhuang; Cast: Wang Renmei (mother of Li Wanli), Liu Yanjin (Hui Sao), Wang Zhelan (Li Wanli), Li Mengyao (Lao Hui), Zhao Wande (Xiao Liu).

Sources for Wang Renmei's Films

DVDs
San Francisco Silent Film Festival
833 Market Street
San Francisco, CA 94103
www.silentfilm.org

VCDs
www.YesAsia.com

35 mm
China Film Archive
No. 3, Wenhuiyuan Road, Xiaoxitian
Haidian District
100088 Beijing, China
Fax: 86-10-6225-9315
Email: cfafad@263.net

Bibliography

Books

1995 Pordenone Silent Film Festival Program. Gemona: Le Giornate del Cinema Muto, 1995.

1997 Pordenone Silent Film Festival Program. Gemona: Le Giornate del Cinema Muto, 1997.

Bailey, Paul J. *China in the Twentieth Century*. Oxford and New York: Basil Blackwell, 1988.

Bailey, Paul J. *China in the Twentieth Century*. Second Edition. Oxford and Malden, MA: Blackwell Publishers, Ltd., 2001.

Baum, Richard. *Burying Mao: Chinese Politics in the Age of Deng Xiaoping*. Princeton, NJ: Princeton University Press, 1994.

Baum, Richard (ed.) *China in Ferment: Perspectives on the Cultural Revolution*. Englewood Cliffs, NJ: Prentice-Hall Inc., 1971.

Berry, Chris. *Chinese Cinema*. Worcester: The Trinity Press, 1991.

Berry, Chris (ed.) *Perspectives on Chinese Cinema*. London: British Film Institute, 1991.

Bisson, T. A. *Japan in China*. New York: The Macmillan Company, 1938.

Browne, Jeremy, and Paul G. Pickowicz. *Dilemmas of Victory*. Cambridge, MA: Harvard University Press, 2007.

Browne, Nick, Paul G. Pickowicz, Vivian Sobchak, and Esther Yau. *New Chinese Cinemas: Forms, Identities, Politics*. Cambridge: Cambridge University Press, 1994.

Chang, Jung, and Jon Halliday. *Mao: The Unknown Story*. New York: Alfred A. Knopf, 2005.

Cheng, Jim. *An Annotated Bibliography for Chinese Film Studies*. Hong Kong: Hong Kong University Press, 2004.

Chow, Rey. *Primitive Passions: Visuality, Sexuality, Ethnography of Contemporary Chinese Cinema*. New York: Columbia University Press, 1995.

Clark, Paul. *Chinese Cinema: Culture and Politics Since 1949*. Cambridge: Cambridge University Press, 1987.

Clark, Paul. *Reinventing China: A Generation and Its Films*. Hong Kong: The Chinese University Press, 2005.

Coble, Parks, M. Jr. *The Shanghai Capitalists and the Nationalist Movement, 1927–1937*. Second edition. Cambridge, MA and London, England: Council on East Asian Studies, Harvard University, 1986.

de Crespigny, R. R. C. *China This Century*. Sydney: Thomas Nelson (Australia), Ltd., 1975.

Dong, Stella. *Shanghai: The Rise and Fall of a Decadent City*. New York: Harper Collins, 2000.

Eastman, Lloyd E. *Seeds of Destruction: Nationalist China in War and Revolution*. Stanford: Stanford University Press, 1984.

Eastman, Lloyd E. *The Abortive Revolution: China Under Nationalist Rule, 1927–1937*. Third Printing. Cambridge, MA: Howard University Press, 1990.

Eastman, Lloyd E., Jerome Ch'en, Suzanne Pepper, and Lyman P. Van Slyke. *The Nationalist Era in China*. Cambridge: *1927–1949*. Cambridge University Press, 1991.

Ehrlich, Linda C., and David Dosser. *Cinematic Landscapes: Observations on the Visual Arts and Cinema of China and Japan*. Austin: The University of Texas Press, 1994.

Encyclopedia of Chinese Films. Volumes 1 (1905–1930), 2 (1931–1949), 3 (1949.10–1976). Beijing: China Movie Publishing House, 1996.

Fu, Poshek. *Passivity, Resistance and Collaborators: Intellectual Choices in Occupied Shanghai, 1937–1945*. Austin: University of Texas Press, 1997.

Fu, Poshek. *Between Shanghai and Hong Kong*. Stanford: Stanford University Press, 2003.

Fu, Poshek, and David Dressen (eds.). *The Cinema of Hong Kong: History, Arts, Identity*. Cambridge and New York: Cambridge University Press, 2000.

Gasster, Michael. *China's Struggle to Modernize*. New York: McGraw-Hill, 1983.

Gernet, Jacques. *A History of Chinese Civilization*. Cambridge, NY: Cambridge University Press, 1996.

Hu, Jubin. *Projecting a Nation: Chinese National Cinema Before 1949*. Hong Kong: Hong Kong University Press, 2003.

Hutchings, Graham. *Modern China: A Guide to a Century of Change*. Cambridge, MA: Howard University Press, 2001.

Jones, Andrew F. *Yellow Music*. Durhan and London: Duke University Press, 2001.

Knoshu, Harry H. *Celluloid China: Cinematic Encounters with Culture and Society*. Carbondale: Southern Illinois University Press, 2002.

Law, Kar (ed.) *Early Images of Hong Kong and China*. Hong Kong: The Urban Council, 1995.

Lee, Leo Ou-fan. *Shanghai Modern: The Flowering of a New Urban Culture in China, 1930–1945*. Cambridge, MA: Harvard University Press, 1999.

Leyda, Jay. *Dianying, Electric Shadows: An Account of Films and the Film Audience in China*. Cambridge, MA: The MIT Press, 1972.

Li, Jui. *The Early Revolutionary Activities of Comrad Mao Tse-Tung*. Translated by Anthony W. Sariti, and edited by James C. Hsiung. White Plains, NY: M.E. Sharpe, Inc., 1977.

Li, Suyuan, and Hu Jubin. *Chinese Silent Film History*. Beijing: China Film Press, 1997.

Lu, Sheldon Hsiao-peng. *Transnational Chinese Cinemas*. Honolulu: University of Hawaii Press, 1999.

Marion, Donald J. *The Chinese Filmography*. Jefferson, NC: McFarland and Company, 1997.

Meyer, Richard J. *Ruan Ling-yu: The Goddess of Shanghai*. Hong Kong: Hong Kong University Press, 2005.

Meyer, Richard J. *Jin Yan: The Rudolph Valentino of Shanghai*. Hong Kong: Hong Kong University Press, 2009.

Moise, Edwin E. *Modern China: A History*. London and New York: Longman, 1986.

Mosely, George. *China Since 1911*. New York, Evanston: Harper and Row Publishers, 1968.

Murowchick, Robert E. *China: Ancient Culture, Modern Land (Cradles of Civilization)*. Norman, OK: University of Oklahoma Press, 1994.

Pang, Laikwan. *Building a New China in Cinema: The Chinese Left-Wing Movement, 1932–1937*. Lanhan, MD: Rowman and Littlefield Publishers, Inc., 2002.

Phillips, Richard T. *China Since 1911*. New York: St. Martin's Press, 1996.

Qin, Yi. *I Play All the Roles*. Shanghai: Shanghai Press, 1997.

Rayns, Tony, and Scott Meek (eds.). *Electric Shadows: 45 Years of Chinese Cinema*. London: BFI, 1980.

Rummel, R.J. *China's Bloody Century: Genocide and Mass Murder since 1900*. New Brunswick: Transaction Publishers, 1991.

Schoppa, R. Keith. *The Columbia Guide to Modern Chinese History*. New York: Columbia University Press, 2000.

Schram, Stuart. *Mao Tse-tung*. Second printing. New York: Simon and Schuster, 1966.

Schwarcz, Vera. *The Chinese Enlightenment: Intellectuals and the Legacy of the May Fourth Movement of 1919*. Berkeley, Los Angeles and London: University of California Press, 1986.

Sensel, George S., Hong Xia, and Ping Jian (eds.). *Chinese Film Theory*. New York: Praeger, 1990.

Sergeant, Harriet. *Shanghai*. London: Jonathan Cape, 1991.

Shaffer, Lynda. *Mao and the Workers, the Hunan Labor Movement, 1920–1923*. Armonk, New York: M.E. Sharpe, Inc., 1982.

Sheridan, James E. *China in Disintegration: The Republican Era in Chinese History, 1912–1949*. New York: The Free Press/ Macmillan, 1975.

Short, Phillip. *Mao: A Life*. New York: Henry Holt & Company, LLC, 1999.

Silbergeld, Jerome. *China into Film: Frames of Reference in Contemporary Chinese Cinema*. London: Reaktion Books, Ltd., 1999.

Snow, Lois Wheeler. *Edgar Snow's China: A Personal Account of the Chinese Revolution*. New York: Vintage Books, 1983.

Soled, Debra E. (ed.) *China: A Nation in Transition*. Washington, DC: Congressional Quarterly Inc., 1995.

Spence, Jonathan D. *The Gate of Heavenly Peace: The Chinese and Their Revolution, 1895–1980*. New York: Viking Press, 1981.

Spence, Jonathan D. *The Search for Modern China*. New York and London: W.W. Norton and Company, 1990.

Tam, Kwok-kan, and Wimal Dissanayake. *New Chinese Cinema*. Hong Kong: Oxford University Press, 1998.

Terrill, Ross. *A Biography: Mao*. New York: Harper and Row Publishers, 1980.

Tien, Hung-mao. *Government and Politics in KMT China, 1927–1937*. Stanford: Stanford University Press, 1972.

Tuchman, Barbara W. *Stillwell and the American Experience in China, 1911–1945*. New York: Macmillan, 1970.

Vogel, Esra F. *Deng Xiaoping and the Transformation of China*. Cambridge, MA and London, England: The Belknap Press of Harvard University Press, 2011.

Wakemen, Frederick, Jr. *Policing Shanghai, 1927–1937*. Berkeley, Los Angeles, London: University of California Press, 1995.

Wang, Renmei. *Memoir: Wo de chengming yu buxing*, edited by Xie Bo. Shanghai: Shanghai Art Press [Shanghai: Wenyi Chubanshe], 1985.

Wang, Y. C. *Chinese Intellectuals and the West, 1872–1949*. Chapel Hill: University of North Carolina Press, 1966.

Widmer, Ellen, and David Der-wei Wang (eds.). *From May Fourth to June Fourth: Fiction and Film in Twentieth-Century China*. Cambridge, MA: Harvard University Press, 1993.

Xin, Jianfei. *Mao Zedong's World View: From Youth to Yan'an*. Lanham, MD and Oxford, UK: University Press of America, Inc., 1998.

Zhang, Yingjin. *The City in Modern Chinese Literature and Film: Configurations of Space, Time, and Gender*. Stanford, CA: Stanford University Press, 1996.

Zhang, Yingjin. *Chinese National Cinema*. New York, London: Routledge, 2004.

Zhang, Yingjin (ed.) *Cinema and Urban Culture in Shanghai, 1922–1943*. Stanford: Stanford University Press, 1999.

Zhang, Yingjin, and Xiao Zhiwei. *Encyclopedia of Chinese Film*. London and New York: Routledge, 1998.

Zhang, Zhen. *An Amorous History of the Silver Screen: Shanghai Cinema, 1896–1937*. Chicago and London: The University of Chicago Press, 2005.

Articles and Periodicals

Baum, Richard. "Ideology Redivivus." In Richard Baum (ed.), *China in Ferment: Perspectives on the Cultural Revolution*. Englewood Cliffs, NJ: Prentice-Hall Inc., 1971, pp. 60–66.

Bergère, Marie-Claire. "'The Other China': Shanghai from 1919 to 1949." In Christopher Howe (ed.), *Shanghai: Revolution and Development in an Asian Metropolis*. Cambridge: Cambridge University Press, 1981, pp. 7–9.

Berry, Chris. "Films of the Cultural Revolution." *Journal of Asian Culture*, VI: 1982, pp. 37–72.

Bo, Xie, "Preface." In Wang Renmei, *Memoir: Wo de chengming yu buxing*, edited by Xie Bo. Shanghai: Shanghai Art Press [Shanghai: Wenyi Chubanshe], 1985, pp. 284–285.

Bridgham, Philip. "Mao's Cultural Revolution: Origin and Development" (part 2). In Richard Baum (ed.), *China in Ferment: Perspectives on the Cultural Revolution*. Englewood Cliffs, NJ: Prentice-Hall, Inc., 1971, pp. 1–35.

Caesar, Diane. "Chinese Film: Sources and Resources." *Cinema Journal* 34, No. 4, Summer 1995, pp. 83–88.

Cheng Jihua, Li Shubai, and Xing Zuwen. "Chinese Cinema: Catalogue of Films, 1905–1937," *Griffithiana*, 54, October 1995, p. 41.

"The Chinese Film Industry." *The People's Tribune* IX, April 1, XXIV, 1935, pp. 25–33.

"Decision of the Central Committee of the Chinese Communist Party Concerning the Great Proletarian Cultural Revolution." *Peking Review*, No. 33, August 12, 1966, pp. 6–11.

"Diary of Li Minwei." *Dazhong Dianying*, August 2003, No. 15, pp. 44–45.

Franz, Michael. "The Struggle for Power." In Richard Baum (ed.), *China in Ferment: Perspectives on the Cultural Revolution.* Englewood Cliffs, NJ: Prentice-Hall, Inc., 1971, pp. 12–21.

Fu, Poshek. "Between Nationalism and Colonialism: Mainland Émigrés, Marginal Culture, and Hong Kong Cinema, 1937–1941." In Poshek Fu and David Desser (eds.), *The Cinema of Hong Kong: History, Arts, Identity*. Cambridge: Cambridge University Press, 2000, pp. 199–226.

He Ling (Shi Linghe). "Sun Yu: His Life and Films." *Zhonghua Tuhua Zazhi* [China Picture Magazine], No. 45, August 1936, in *Griffithiana*, 60/61, October 1997, pp. 155–161.

Horowitz, Stephen. "Brief History of the Chinese Cinema." *American Film Institute China Week Brochure*, 1981, p. 1.

Kerlan-Stephens. "The Making of Modern Icons: Three Actresses of the Lianhua Film Company." *European Journal of East Asian Studies*, June 2007, pp. 43–73.

Lee, Leo Ou-fan. "Urban Milieu of Shanghai Cinema." In Yingjin Zhang (ed.), *Cinema and Urban Culture in Shanghai, 1922–1943*. Stanford: Stanford University Press, 1999, p. 85.

"Leftist Chinese Cinema of the Thirties." *Cineaste* XVII, No. 3, 1990.

Leyda, Jay. "China Enters the International Film World." *American Film Institute China Week Brochure*, 1981, p. 2.

Li, H. C. "Chinese Electric Shadows: A Selected Bibliography of Materials in English." *Modern Chinese Literature*, Vol. 7, 1993, pp. 117–153.

Mishra, Pankag. "Staying Power: Mao and the Maoists." *The New Yorker,* December 20 and 27, 2010, book section, 5 pages.

Pickowicz, Paul. "Melodramatic Representation and the 'May Fourth' Tradition of Chinese Cinema." In Ellen Widmer and David Derwei Wang (eds.), *From May Fourth to June Fourth: Fiction and Film in Twentieth-Century China.* Cambridge, MA: Harvard University Press, 1993, pp. 295–326.

Pickowicz, Paul G. "Acting Like Revolutionaries: Shi Hui, the Wenhua Studio, and Private-Sector Filmmaking, 1949–1952." In Jeremy Browne and Paul G. Pickowicz (eds.), *Dilemmas of Victory: The Early Years of the People's Republic of China.* Cambridge, MA: Harvard University Press, 2007.

Rayns, Tony. "Early Images of Hong Kong and China." In Law Kar (ed.), *Early Images of Hong Kong and China.* Hong Kong: The Urban Council, 1995, p. 110.

Shih, Joan Chung-wen. "Dominant Themes and Values in Chinese Films." *American Film Institute China Week Brochure*, 1981, p. 3.

Tannenbaum, Gerald. "China's Cultural Revolution: Why It Had to Happen." In Richard Baum (ed.), *China in Ferment: Perspectives on the Cultural Revolution.* Englewood Cliffs, NJ: Prentice-Hall, Inc., 1971, pp. 60–66.

Vincent, Jean-Louis. "Life in Peking: Report from a Long Nose." *The NY Times Magazine*, February 26, 1967.

Wakeman, Fredrick Jr. "Clean-up the New Order in Shanghai." In Jeremy Browne and Paul G. Pickowicz, *Dilemmas of Victory.* Cambridge, MA: Harvard University Press, 2007.

Xia Yan. "Remember the Past as a Lesson for the Future," translated by Fong Kenk Ho, *Dianying Yishu*, No. 1, 1979. In Tony Rayns and Scott Meek (eds.), *Electric Shadows: 45 Years of Chinese Cinema*. London: BFI, 1980, pp. 10–13.

Zhang, Zhen. "Teahouse, Shadowplay, Bricolage: Laborer's Love and the Question of Early Chinese Cinema." In Yingjin Zhang (ed.), *Cinema and Urban Culture in Shanghai, 1922–1943*. Stanford: Stanford University Press, 1999, pp. 27–50.

Newspapers

The New York Times, June 14, 1942.
Renmin Ribao (People's Daily), May 28, 1952.

Interviews

Yuhua Dong, June 12, 2011.
Qin Yi, July 4, 2009.
Dr. Wang Yong, March 26, 2010.

Unpublished Works

Hu, Jubin. "Chinese National Cinema Before 1949." Unpublished PhD dissertation, School of Communication, Arts, and Critical Enquiry, La Trobe University, Australia, 2001.

Pickowicz, Paul G., and Nien Ch'Ao Yu. "Political and Ideological Themes in Chinese Films of the Early Sixties: A Review Essay." Workshop on Contemporary Chinese Literature and the Performing Arts, John King Fairbank Center for East Asian Research, Harvard University, June 12–20, 1979.

Other Materials

Choi, Kai-kwong. *Lai Man-wai: Father of Hong Kong Cinema.* DVD. Hong Kong: Dragon Ray Motion Pictures, Ltd., 2001.
Wild Rose. DVD. San Francisco: San Francisco Silent Film Festival, 2009.

About the Author

R ichard J. Meyer teaches film at Seattle University and is a visiting scholar at the New Zealand Film Archive. He was a distinguished fellow at the Center for Film, Media and Popular Culture at Arizona State University in 2007 and the Distinguished Fulbright Professor at I'Universita' del Piemonte Orientale Amedeo Avogadro in Italy for the spring 2005 trimester. Dr. Meyer is Edmund F. and Virginia B. Ball Professor of Telecommunications Emeritus at Ball State University in Muncie, Indiana and a visiting professor at the Center for Journalism and Media Studies at the University of Hong Kong.

In 2001, he was a fellow of the Asian Cultural Council in Hong Kong. Prior to his appointment to the endowed chair, he was Fulbright Scholar at National Chengchi University in Taiwan where he studied Chinese silent films at the Beijing, Shanghai, Taipei, and Hong Kong Film Archives. Dr. Meyer received his BA and MA degrees from Stanford University and his Ph.D. from New York University. His postdoctoral fellowships were at Columbia University and the East-West Center in Honolulu.

While pursuing a career in public broadcasting as a producer and executive with WNET, New York and CEO at KCTS Seattle and KERA/KDTN Dallas, he maintained a passion for film by experimenting with the medium, as noted by *TV Guide* in April, 1969. He has published in *Public Opinion Quarterly, Journal of Broadcasting, Educational Broadcasting Review, Film Comment, NEA Journal, Time (Asia)* and other periodicals and books. His chapter "Blacks and Broadcasting" appears in the book, *Broadcasting and Bargaining,* published by the University of Wisconsin Press. His section on "The Films of David Wark Griffith" is featured in *Focus on D. W. Griffith*, published by Prentice-Hall. His piece "Reaction to the 'Blue Book'" is presented in *American Broadcasting,* published by Hastings House.

Dr. Meyer has written about the Pordenone International Silent Film Festival for *American Way Magazine*, the *Dallas Morning News*, and other publications. In addition, he has produced two CDs: "Piano Themes from the Silent Screen" and "Piano Portraits of the Goddess," and three DVDs: the 1934 classic Chinese film, *The Goddess*; the 1931 Shanghai hit, *The Peach Girl*; and *Wild Rose*, one of the most popular films of the 1930s. His books, *Ruan Lingyu: The Goddess of Shanghai* and *Jin Yan: The Rudolph Valentino of Shanghai,* were published by Hong Kong University Press in 2005 and 2009 respectively.

Throughout the United States, Asia, Southern Africa, and Europe, Dr. Meyer has been a broadcasting consultant, technical and media advisor to public and private schools, cultural groups, the State University of New York, UNESCO, the Corporation for Public Broadcasting, the United States Information Agency, and various radio and television institutions. He has worked in all phases of film and educational television production.

The series "Communications and Education," on which he served as executive producer, won the Ohio State Award in 1968. His film, *The Garden of Eden*, was responsible, in part, for saving the Garden of Eden in Lucas, Kansas. He has been a speaker at the Buster Keaton Celebration, the Taiwan International Symposium on Public Media, the International Film Studies Conference, the International Federation of Film Archives (FIAF) Congress, and numerous venues about film and broadcasting.

Dr. Meyer was a member of the President's Communications Council at Howard University, an associate of the Columbia University's seminar on public communications, and an adjunct professor at Simon Fraser University in British Columbia, the University of Texas at Dallas and the University of North Texas. He was a member of the board of directors of the National Association of Educational Broadcasters, the board of managers of the Public Broadcasting Service, the board of directors of the Public Broadcasting Service, and the president of the Washington Educational Network. He served on the Executive Committee of the American Program Service, the Executive Board of the Meadows School of the Arts at Southern Methodist University, and as a member of the National Advisory Council of the Van Cliburn International Piano Competition and a director of the National Museum of Communications.

Presently, Dr. Meyer is president emeritus of the San Francisco Silent Film Festival and a member of the Board of Directors of the Seattle International Film Festival. He produces and introduces restored silent films accompanied by music at various "LIVE CINEMA" presentations. He is a certified scuba instructor of the National Association of Underwater Instructors. His underwater photographs and articles about diving have appeared in various magazines.